CANON 16

THE CATHOLIC UNIVERSITY OF AMERICA
CANON LAW STUDIES
NO. 307

CANON 16

A Historical Synopsis and a Commentary

A DISSERTATION

SUBMITTED TO THE FACULTY OF THE SCHOOL OF CANON LAW OF THE CATHOLIC UNIVERSITY OF AMERICA IN PARTIAL FULFILLMENT OF THE REQUIREMENTS FOR THE DEGREE OF DOCTOR IN CANON LAW

BY
REVEREND MICHAEL J. REGAN, J.C.L.
PRIEST OF THE DIOCESE OF ATLANTA

THE CATHOLIC UNIVERSITY OF AMERICA PRESS
WASHINGTON, D. C.
1959

NIHIL OBSTAT:

J. Rogg Schmidt, A.B., J.C.D.

Censor Deputatus

Washingtonii, D. C., die 1 octobris 1958

IMPRIMATUR:

+ Franciscus Eduardus Hyland, D.D., J.C.D.

Episcopus Atlantensis

Atlantae, die 9 novembris 1958

Printed by Harper Printing Co., Inc., Atlanta, Ga.

18

TO

OUR VIRGIN MOTHER OF GOOD COUNSEL

FOREWORD

Inasmuch as man has been endowed by his Creator with an intellect and free will, he is capable of acquiring knowledge and also of increasing in knowledge. Man does not come into this world with innate ideas. His knowledge comes to him indirectly, i.e., through his senses; and needless to say, his knowledge is acquired gradually. Canon 88, § 3, contains the presumption that a child has arrived at the use of reason upon the completion of his seventh year.

The faculty of intellect is regarded by the Thomistic philosophers as human nature's primary prerogative. But this superior faculty of intellect is restricted within a nature which is finite, which means therefore that the scope of human knowledge is necessarily limited. Furthermore the intellect of each individual is distinguished from that of every other human being and indeed from all others—past, present and to come—by the particular physical body in which the particular intellect resides. The human intellect is also in a weakened and darkened condition because of the fall of the father of the human family, Adam. Indeed, a profound mystery is involved as regards man's ability to know and the extent of his knowledge.

Since man is by nature limited as to the operation and capacity of his faculty of intellect, it follows conversely that he is constituted by nature in a state of ignorance. It is evident also that man is prone to fall into intellectual error because he has inherited a fallen nature. Human ignorance and error are necessary concomitants of man's imperfect state of being. They are contingent likewise upon the indirect manner in which he acquires knowledge.

Canon 16, which is the object of this study, contains two paragraphs both of which legislate concerning ignorance. The first paragraph of this canon expresses the legal principle that no ignorance excuses from invalidating and disqualifying laws unless the law itself expressly states otherwise. The second paragraph of the canon enunciates five presumptions of law. The first four of these presumptions deny that ignorance or error is presumed in any of the four following instances: in regard to the law; in regard to the penalty attached to the law; in regard to one's own actions or experiences (*facta propria*); and finally, in regard to *notorious* facts of others (persons or things). The fifth presumption, however, admits ignorance in regard to *non-notorious* facts of others (persons or things).

The present study is divided into two sections: the historical treatment and the canonical commentary. In the historical part the author has tried to assemble the principles and rules from a variety of widely separated sources in an effort to indicate the origins and development of the elements contained in canon 16. Moreover, since canon 16 is a restatement of the law before the Code, it was necessary to refer constantly to the pre-Code legislation throughout the canonical commentary. The author has also tried to avoid as diligently as possible the subject of ignorance in relation to imputability. The latter subject is treated completely and in a most scholarly manner in a dissertation by the Rev. Innocent R. Swoboda, O.F.M., J.C.D. Father Swoboda's work proved to be an invaluable aid in the present study, and the author wishes to express his heartfelt gratitude and appreciation for so helpful a reference.

The writer prepared the present work during the years 1947 to 1949 while he was a student in the School of Canon Law at the Catholic University, and the dissertation was approved by the Faculty for publication at that time. Since almost ten years have passed since the completion of the work, the writer respectfully requests the readers of the dissertation to take the circumstances of its publication into consideration.

The writer was assigned by His Eminence, Dennis Cardinal Dougherty, the late Archbishop of Philadelphia, to pursue the study of Canon Law at the Catholic University of America. The writer wishes to acknowledge his debt of profound gratitude to His Eminence, the late Archbishop of Philadelphia, for the opportunity afforded him to pursue advance studies in Canon Law. He is also particularly indebted to the Faculty of the School of Canon Law at the Catholic University of America, Washington,

D. C., for its kind guidance and patient direction. He likewise expresses humble thanks and deepest gratitude to His Excellency, Most Rev. Francis E. Hyland, D.D., J.C.D., first Bishop of the Diocese of Atlanta, for his encouragement and assistance in the publication of this work.

TABLE OF CONTENTS

PAGE

CHAPTER VI

CHAPTER VII

PART ONE

Historical Synopsis

CHAPTER 1

IGNORANCE IN ROMAN LAW

Since the legislation of canon 16 is dependent in a remarkable manner upon the Roman Law norms, concepts and principles in regard to ignorance and error, the historical background of canon 16 would be incomplete unless some consideration were given to Roman Law, which is in the ultimate analysis the basis of this canon. Although the Roman Law sources do not offer a specific treatment of ignorance regarding invalidating and disqualifying laws as they are understood in the present day, nevertheless they contain many examples of ignorance and error in respect to the law, to the penalty attached to the law, to one's own acts, and to both the notorious and non-notorious actions of others. The sources likewise point to the general presumption of knowledge regarding law and fact, and they indicate moreover that whenever ignorance is alleged the same must be proved.

The following articles present in rudimentary form the attitude of the Roman legalistic mind toward ignorance and error in the aforementioned aspects.

ARTICLE 1. THE SUBJECTIVE ELEMENT IN THE VIOLATION OF LAW— *Dolus* and *Culpa*

The primitive law of Rome seemed to look only to the material and objective violation of law, almost completely irrespective of the state of mind of the agent.[1] Indeed most legal systems in the initial stages of their development tend to be particularly formalistic and rigorous. Legal institutions are regarded not as means to an end but as an end in themselves. The adaptability of law comes about only after many years of enforcement.

[1] H. F. Jolowicz, *Historical Introduction to the Study of Roman Law* (Cambridge: University Press, 1932), pp. 177-178.

It must be said, however, that the realistic Roman mind, from quite an early date, considered the subjective elements entering into the violation of law, namely, the knowledge and deliberation of the agent. Thus some of the earliest historical Roman Law records indicated a distinction between homicide committed *"dolo sciens"* and *"si quis imprudens occidisset hominem."*[2] Later on, moreover, this distinction between the intentional *(dolus)* and unintentional violation of law was developed further, namely, when infractions of law committed through culpable negligence *(culpa)* became the objects of a distinct legal consideration. The deliberate violation of law according to the Romans was expressed in various terms. Among the most frequently used are: *"dolo sciens,"*[3] *"sciens dolo malo,"*[4] *dolo malo"*[5] and several other relatively equivalent expressions.

The *Digest* contains two definitions of *"dolus"* in reference to purely civil matters.[6] A definition of criminal *"dolus"* is not given; consequently the exact meaning of this type of *"dolus"* has been the object of considerable speculation among Romanists. The solution of this difficult proposition rests with the specialists

---

[2] P. Girard, *Textes de Droit Romain* (5. ed., Paris: Rosseau, 1923), p. 8.

[3] Girard, *Textes de Droit Romain*, p. 8.

[4] Lex Latina Tabulae Bantinae (621-636 A.U.C.)—C. Bruns, *Fontes Iuris Romani Antiqui* (7. ed. ab O. Gradenwitz, Tubingae, 1909), 1, 54 (hereafter this work will be cited as Bruns, *Fontes*); Lex Acilia Repetundarum (621-632 A.U.C.)—Bruns, *Fontes*, I, 60; D. (48, 15) 3, pr. (Lex Fabia de plagiariis); D. (48, 10) (9, 3) (Lex Cornelia de falsis).

[5] D. (48, 12) (2, 1) (*Lex Iulia de annona*); D. (48, 10) (9, 2) (Lex Cornelia de falsis); D. (47, 12) 3, pr. (de sepulchro violato).

[6] ". . . dolus malus fit calliditate et fallacia: et ut ait Pedius, dolo malo pactum fit, quotiens circumscribendi alterius causa aliud agitur et aliud agi simulatur. "—D. (2, 14) (7, 9). "Dolum malum Servius quidem ita definiit: machinationem quandam alterius decipiendi causa, cum aliud simulatur et aliud agitur. Labeo autem posse et sine simultatione id agi, ut quis circumveniatur; . . . itaque ipse sic definiit dolum malum esse omnem calliditatem fallaciam machinationem ad circumveniendum fallendum decipiendum alterum adhibitam. "—D. (4, 3) (1, 2).

in Roman Law.[7] It seems sufficiently apparent, however, that criminal *"dolus"* did not imply the notion of secret or crafty malice,[8] nor did it imply an idea of premeditation and the wilful contempt of law and justice.[9]

Thus *"dolus"* may be defined as the simple deliberate performance of a prohibited act. Clear knowledge or the contempt of the law was not implied. This conclusion, namely, that *"dolus"* consisted in the simple will to commit an injury, is further strengthened when one considers that the Ruman jurists used such expressions as *"animus occidendi"*[10] and *"voluntas nocendi"*[11] instead of the word *"dolus."* Mommsen (1817-1903)[12] defined *"dolus"* as comprising *"toute les illegalites conscientes,"* and Ferrini (1859-1902) described it as *"l'intenzione consciente di nuocere."*[13] However, the meaning of *"dolus"* may have changed during the periods of Roman Law history.[14]

As a member of society man must not only positively avoid inflicting injury, but he must also take proper precautions that his actions, however legitimate, do not cause harm to others. Consequently, he must guard against the negligence connoted in *"culpa."*[15] Thus according to the *"Lex Aquilia"*[16] an owner was authorized to initiate legal proceedings against someone who through negligence had damaged his property, generally slaves.

---

[7] Cf. A. Pernice, "Der verbrecherische Vorsatz im griechisch-römischen Rechte," *Zeitschrift der Savigny-Stiftung für Rechtsgeschichte: Romanistische Abteilung,* XVIII (1896), 205-251; C. Ferrini, *Diritto Penale Romano* (Milano, 1899), pp. 78-103; G. Falchi, *Diritto Penale Romano* (Treviso: Vianello, 1930), pp. 87-99.

[8] Binding's theory (Normen und ihre Uebertretung [Leipzig, 1872-1888], II, 278)—Ferrini, *Diritto Penale Romano,* p. 79.

[9] Ferrini (*op. cit.,* pp. 79-80) ascribed this theory to Leist, *Gräco-Italische Rechtsgeschichte,* p. 370.

[10] D. (48, 8) (1, 3).

[11] C. (9, 16) 1.

[12] *Droit Pénal Romain* (trans. by J. Duquesne, 3 vols., Paris, 1907), I, 100.

[13] *Op. cit.,* p. 89.

[14] Cf. Falchi, *Diretto Penale Romano,* pp. 87-95.

[15] "Magna negligentia culpa est."—D. (50, 16) 226.

[16] D. (9, 2); cf. Gaius, *Institutiones,* (3, 211), (4, 3) 3; D. (9, 2) (5, 1).

"Culpa" could also exist in the logical order; it was considered gross negligence (*lata culpa*) not to know what all persons know.[17]

ARTICLE 2. IGNORANCE IN GENERAL

The most fundamental division of ignorance in Roman Law was founded on the unknown object. When this unknown object was the law itself the Romans used the designation ignorance of law (*ignorantia iuris*), but when the object was not the law itself but something unknown in its objective and factual elements as constituting a violation of law, then the ignorance was called ignorance of fact (*ignorantia facti*).

The jurists,[18] the *Digest,*[19] as well as the *Code of Justinian*[20] treated of this obviously important and constantly emphasized distinction. Unfortunately, however, the sources do not contain a definition of either of these far-reaching and important classes of ignorance. The jurists merely furnished a number of examples of this division. From the instances they mention, one can describe ignorance of law as a lack of knowledge concerning the law itself, the contents of the law, the meaning of the law, or the extension of the law, whereas ignorance of fact connoted the failure to grasp certain objective or factual circumstances as constituting a violation of law[21].

---

[17] "Latae culpae finis est non intelligere id quod omnes intelligunt,"—D. (50, 16) 223. The *Glossa Ordinaria* commentators expressed this law in the words, ". . . nulli licet ignorare quae publice facta sunt."—*Glossa Ordinaria* ad. pr. D. XXXVIII, s. v. *cum itaque*, ad c. 14, D. XVI.

[18] V. gr., Paulus, in his *Liber Singularis de iuris et facti ignorantia*—D. (22, 9) pr.

[19] D. (22, 6).

[20] C. (1, 18).

[21] The expression *"ignorantia iuris"* designated the objective law, not the subjective right (*ius subiectivum*). Therefore, *"ius ignorare"* or *"ignorantia iuris"* was not the same as *"ius suum ignorare"* or *"de iure suo ignorare."* The latter connoted not ignorance of law but ignorance of fact, i.e., a lack of knowledge in regard to the facts of one's juridical condition. Consequently in the text of D. (22, 6) 3, pr.: "Plurimum interest, utrum quis de alterius causa et facto non sciret an de iure suo ignorat," the distinction was not between *"ignorantia iuris et facti,"* but between *"ignorantia facti proprii"* and *"ignorantia*

One finds in the Roman Law sources an extensive treatment of error in reference to contracts. Every contract in Roman Law consisted of two essential elements: the agreement of the parties (*pactum*), and secondly a legal reason (*causa*) why the agreement ought to be enforced by law.[22] The agreement consisted in an accord of the wills of the contracting parties.[23]

Although the sources do not explicitly distinguish between substantial and accidental error, nevertheless, several examples indicate that the distinction was made in practice.[24] Thus an error in respect to the identity of a person rendered a contract null and void as, for example, when a person agreed to lend money to a certain party who was thought to be some other person. In such a case the contract of *mutuum* was not entered into. Accidental error, e.g., error of quality, was of no consequence in this instance.[25]

The same was true when someone contracted to sell silver for gold, or when one agreed to buy a particular slave, and another one was delivered in his place. Such contracts were rendered invalid.[26]

In other matters, however, the Roman jurists seem to use the terms ignorance and error interchangeably. Thus in the Code of Justinian, laws which treated of ignorance and error were classified under the title, "*De iuris et facti ignorantia.*"[27]

---

facti alieni." Cf. F. K. Savigny, *System des heutigen römischen Rechts* (8 vols., Berlin, 1840-1949), III, 327; Swoboda, *Ignorance in Relation to the Imputability of Delicts*, The Catholic University of America Canon Law Studies, N. 143 (Washington, D. C.: The Catholic University of America Press, 1941), p. 7, footnote n. 23.

[22] Cf. R. W. Leage, *Roman Private Law* (2. ed., by C. H. Ziegler, London: Macmillan and Co., 1946), p. 346.

[23] Cf. P. Girard, *Manuel Elémentaire de Droit Romain* (7. ed., Paris, 1924), p. 479; C. Ferrini, *Manuale di Pandette* (3. ed., Milano, 1917), n. 166.

[24] Cf. W. W. Buckland, *A Text-Book of Roman Law* (Cambridge, 1921), p. 412.

[25] D. (18, 2), (14, 3); cf. Girard, *op. cit.* p. 480.

[26] D. (2, 14) (1, 2); Buckland, *op. cit.*, p. 412; Ferrini, *op. cit.*, n. 168.

[27] C. (1, 18).

ARTICLE 3. IGNORANCE OF THE LAW

Ignorance of the law as given in the foregoing article may be defined as the lack of knowledge concerning the law itself, its content, its meaning or its scope. Until quite recently it was generally held that ignorance of those laws to which a penalty was attached did not excuse.[28] But whatever may have been the true doctrine of the classical Roman Law, the *Code of Justinian* did not consider ignorance of law as an excuse from penal liability; whenever it treated of ignorance of law and ignorance of fact, the latter indeed was said to excuse, but not the former.[29] The medieval canonists generally agreed that ignorance of law did not excuse, and they expressly referred to Roman Law in support of this opinion.

Kantorowicz (1877-1940) held that the Roman Law did not make a distinction between natural or quasi-natural law (*ius gentium*) and civil law so far as ignorance was concerned.[30] Although Roman Law did not punish the mere objective violation of law without regard for the subjective elements in the violation of law, nevertheless in the generality of cases ignorance of law was not admitted, since most of the penal laws had a foundation in the natural law.[31]

Ignorance of the natural law and of the *"ius gentium"* did not excuse, for there existed the general presumption that anyone capable of *"dolus"* had also a knowledge of these laws. Thus even women, who were generally presumed ignorant of the law,[32]

---

[28] Cf. Ferrini, *Diritto Penale Romano*, pp. 144-152.

[29] V. gr.: ". . . ignorantia enim excusatur non iuris, sed facti."—D. (3, 2) 11, 4: Regula est iuris quidem ignorantiam cuique nocere, facti vera ignorantiam non nocere."—D. (22, 6) 9.

[30] Hermann Kantorowicz with the collaboration of W. W. Buckland, *Studies in the Glossators of Roman Law* (Cambridge: University Press, 1938), p. 79. This author admitted, however, that at least from the time of Bulgarus (d. 1166) the distinction was made by the glossators and commentators of Roman Law.

[31] Cf. Falchi, *Diretto Penale Romano*, pp. 109-110; Mommsen-Duquesne, *Droit Pénal Romain*, I, 108.

[32] ". . . ius ignorare permissum est. quod et in feminis in quibusdam causis propter sexus infirmitatem dicitur: et ideo sicubi non est delictum, sed iuris ignorantia, non laeduntur."—D. (22, 6) 9.

could not allege ignorance as an excuse from the natural law or the *"ius gentium."*[33]

The denial of ignorance of the law was not restricted to laws of a penal character. An imperial decree (circa 385) stated that an understanding of the most sacred laws which control the lives of men had to be possessed by all persons, so that, with a universal knowledge of the legal provisions, men might avoid what is forbidden and observe what is permitted.[34] A few years later (391) the Emperors Valentinian II (375-392) and Theodosius I (379-395) in a decree to Flavian, the Praetorian Prefect of Illyricum and Italy, declared that they did not permit anyone to be or to pretend to be ignorant of the Imperial Constitutions.[35] There was an express obligation to know these laws.

In the year 439 the Emperors Theodosius II (408-450) and Valentinian III (425-455) decreed that no act or agreement prohibited by law could be entered into by the contracting parties; furthermore, that it was enough for the legislator merely to prohibit what he did not wish to be done, and that, when something was forbidden by law but nevertheless was done, it should not only be void but be considered as not having been done at all, even though the legislator may have made the prohibition only in general terms and did not expressly state that contrary acts were void. Thus the positive civil legislation which came from the highest lawgiver in the State was universally binding upon all, and all were bound to understand and to conform to the laws which controlled their lives, and any acts performed contrary to them were invalid.[36]

However, certain classes were expressly exempted from this general rule: the unlearned,[37] minors, i.e., those below the age

---

[33] D. (48, 5) (39, 1, 2).

[34] "Leges sacratissimae, quae constringunt omnium vitas, intelligi ab omnibus debent . . ."—C. (1, 14) 9.

[35] "Constitutiones principum nec ignorare quemquam nec dissimulare permittimus."—C. (1, 18) 12.

[36] C. 1, 14) 5.

[37] D. (22, 3) (25, 1).

of twenty-five,[38] women[39] and soldiers.[40] Thus the law made explicit exception for those who because of their age, sex or occupation could hardly and reasonably be expected to know the law.

Ignorance regarding the laws which originated through local authority and which were peculiar to a particular locality, e.g., municipal laws, was admitted as an exception when the existence of ignorance could be duly established by proof.[41]

During the reign of Justinian (527-565) the praetorian prefect transmitted copies of the imperial constitutions to public officials in the provinces, who in the name of the emperor officially announced the new laws in order that they would be known, understood and observed by the subjects.[42]

ARTICLE 4. IGNORANCE OF FACT

As mentioned above, ignorance of fact connotes the failure to grasp certain objective or factual circumstances as constituting a violation of law. In the Roman legal system ignorance or error of fact generally excused from liability, and this principle was frequently stated in the sources.[43]

In Roman Law provision was made for legitimate ignorance of fact, and a person could win his case upon proving his alleged ignorance. Thus, when through ignorance of fact a person paid money which was not due, he had the right to recover the money provided that proof of his ignorance was furnished.[44] In like manner, if a person alleged that he had paid money which was not due, he was required to produce evidence that the money was paid through the fraud of the party who received it, or in consequence of some just cause of ignorance. Unless he furnished

---

[38] Cf. D. (22, 6) 9; C. (8, 39) 1; (1, 18) 2 and 8.

[39] D. (22, 3) (25, 1).

[40] C. (1, 18) 1.

[41] D. (50, 9) 6.

[42] ". . . ut et tabelliones vim eius cognoscant et subditi eandem intellegant legemque servent."—Novellae (66, 1).

[43] C. (9, 20) 14; D. (47, 2) (46, 7); Inst. (4, 2) 1; C. (1, 18) 4; C. (1, 18) 6; V. (1, 18) 10).

[44] C. (1, 18) 10.

these proofs, however, he had no right to recover the money. Thus the presentation of proof of one's ignorance of fact could outweigh the legal presumption of knowledge.[45]

In order to excuse, the ignorance had to be "*iusta*"[46] or "*probabilis*."[47] Probable ignorance was that ignorance which could not be overcome through a diligent investigation;[48] and since the understanding of facts frequently escaped even the most diligent,[49] a person was not required to exercise the highest degree of diligence.[50]

However, ignorance which was "*crassa*," or "*supina*,"[51] or "*dissoluta*,"[52] or "*captiosa*," did not excuse,[53] since ignorance of this kind was equivalent to "*lata culpa*;" i.e., a lack of knowledge regarding what was generally known. Knowledge which was presumed as common knowledge was that which related to a knowledge of the law and of personal and public facts.[54]

Everyone was presumed to know his own condition and actions, and hence only ignorance of facts relative to a third person (*facta aliena*) was recognized in law.[55] Those who pleaded ignorance or error regarding their own acts were obliged to produce evidence to that effect.[56] If a land owner claimed that he was ignorant of having given his land by way of donation to another, he could obtain a decision in his favor by appearing before a competent judge and there proving that his adversary had, against his consent, contrived to have this inserted in the grant.[57] A person

---

[45] Cf. D. (22, 3) 25.

[46] D. (48, 16) (1, 3); D. (31, 89), 7; D. (50, 17) 42.

[47] D. (41, 10) 5.

[48] D. (50, 17) 42.

[49] D. (22, 6) 2.

[50] ". . . recte Labeo definit scientiam neque curiosissimi . . . hominis accipiendum . . ."—D. (22, 6) 9, 2.

[51] D. (22, 6) 6.

[52] D. (21, 1) 55.

[53] D. (42, 8) (6, 10).

[54] D. (22, 6) (9, 2); D. (47, 9) 11; D. (50, 16) 223.

[55] ". . . quia in alieni facti ignorantia tolerabilis error est."—D. (41, 10) 5; D. (22, 6) 3; D. (50, 18) 42; C. (4, 44) 15.

[56] D. (22, 3) 25; D. (22, 3) (25, 2).

[57] C. (4, 19) 18.

had to furnish proof of his ignorance before he could offset the legal presumption of his possession of knowledge.

CONCLUSION

It follows from the foregoing considerations that the Roman Law system stressed the inviolability of law, and it also set up the general presumption of knowledge of law. Only certain specified categories of persons were accounted as not amenable to this presumption of knowledge. In general, when ignorance was alleged as an excuse, then proof of the existence of ignorance had to be presented and thereupon authoritatively accepted before the excuse was acknowledged. It is evident also that certain aspects of the presumptions in regard to ignorance of fact as contained in canon 16, § 2, had their origin in Roman Law. Thus the presumption against ignorance of *facta aliena notoria* was present in the Roman Law concept of *"culpa."* Moreover, from the foregoing presentation it is clearly indicated that whenever ignorance was alleged it had to be demonstrated.

The Roman Law norms and concepts relative to ignorance and error exerted a far-reaching influence on Canon Law. With the revival of the study of Roman Law in the twelfth century the Canon Law adopted and developed many of these rules of law which have continued in effect to the present day. During the first eleven centuries, however, the Canon Law development on this issue reflected at most a very meager dependence on Roman Law.

CHAPTER II

IGNORANCE IN THE ANCIENT PENITENTIAL SYSTEM UNTIL THE TIME OF GRATIAN (ca. 1140)

The influence of the Christian Church upon the Roman Empire was such that it transformed the civilization of old pagan Rome into a Christian Civilization. Yet the Church also was bound to be influenced in many respects by the culture and the institutions of the Roman Empire. This is especially true as regards the law of the Church as it existed in those times. However, canonical treatises, as we know them today, were not written in the first centuries of Christianity. For the most part the early Christian writers were concerned principally with theological questions. Needless to say, there existed nothing like a detailed treatise or study of invalidating or disqualifying laws in early times. Such was to be the work of later Christian centuries.

ARTICLE 1. THE DOCTRINE OF ST. AUGUSTINE (354-430)

In the writings of St. Augustine we find the concept of error defined as *"existimare scire quod nescit"* and again in the same context as *"approbare falsum"*—an assent of the mind to a false proposition, a positive denial of the objective truth.[1] In regard to that which is not known, he also distinguished between what should be known and what, if known, may prove either harmful or indifferent.[2] St. Augustine did not expressly distinguish between ignorance of law and ignorance of fact. This distinction came into Canon Law much later, and then it was borrowed from the Roman Law. Nevertheless, from the practical solutions he gave,

---

[1] *Enchiridion*, c. 17—Migne, *Patrologiae Cursus Completus, Series Latina*, (221 vols., Parisiis, 1844-1864), XL, 239 (hereafter cited *MPL*); c. 11, D. XXXVIII.

[2] *Loc. cit.*

he seemed to be aware of a difference between these two kinds of ignorance.

St. Augustine did not leave room for any presumption of ignorance relative to the divine law. According to him the divine law remained binding not only for those who positively willed to be ignorant but also for those who simply lacked positive knowledge.[3]

In one of the texts introduced into the *"Decretum Gratiani,"* St. Augustine stated that it is necessary for priests to learn the various branches of ecclesiastical knowledge and discipline, for if a priest is lacking in even one of these respects he is scarcely worthy of the name of priest, since the strict evangelical warning states, "And if the blind lead the blind, both fall into the pit."[4] In the context of St. Augustine's statement this passage implied that priests are not to be presumed ignorant of that knowledge which is required of them in virtue of their state.

ARTICLE 2. THE THEORY AND PRACTICE OF THE ANCIENT DISCIPLINE

From the very beginning the Church in imitation of her Divine Founder[5] upheld the sacrosanct character of law and the salutary purpose enshrined in law.[6]

---

[3] *De Gratia et Libero Arbitrio,* cap. III, n. 5: "Nec tamen ideo confugiendum est ad ignorantiae tenebras, ut in eis quisque requirat excusationem. Aliud est enim nescisse, aliud scire noluisse. Voluntas quippe in eo arguitur, de quo dicitur, 'Noluit intelligere ut bene ageret' (Ps. XXXV, 4). Sed et illa ignorantia quae non est eorum qui scire nolunt, sed eorum qui tanquam simpliciter nesciunt, neminem sic excusat, ut sempiterno igne non ardeat . . . sed fortasse ut mitius ardeat."—*MPL* XLIV, 884-885. Out of this distinction the "*ignorantia invita-simplex-affectata*" division was developed by the Decretists; cf. Swoboda, *Ignorance in Relation to the Imputability of Delicts*, p. 16, note 12.

[4] Matt. 15:14; c. 5, D. XXXVIII; Mansi, *Sacrorum Conciliorum Nova et Amplissima Collectio* (53 vols. in 60, Parisiis, 1901-1927), XIV, 395 (hereafter cited Mansi).

[5] "Do not think that I am come to destroy the law or the prophets. . . . He therefore that shall break one of these least commandments and shall so teach men shall be called the least in the kingdom of heaven." Matt. 5:17, 19.

[6] "That you abstain from things sacrificed to idols and from things

In spite of the difficulties encountered in communications during those days, the popes and bishops exercised supreme care in making their legislation known to the faithful, both clerical and lay. Thus, Tertullian (ca. 160—ca. 230) relates that laws were read in the churches at an early date.[7] Laws pertaining to the clergy were promulgated during the synods in the presence of the clergy and bishops.[8]

The ancient penitential system in the Church gave rise to a body of laws quite different from the highly developed system of present day Canon Law. Like many legal systems in their initial stages, it almost completely submerged the subjective elements involved in the violation of law, namely, the knowledge and deliberation of the agent. Whether this system explicitly provided for the legal presumption of knowledge regarding both law and fact is frequently difficult to determine from the sources.

1. Early Doctrine and Legislation

The *Pastor Hermae* (ca. 140-155) considered the case of a husband who continued to live with an unfaithful wife of whose infidelity he was ignorant. According to the penitential discipline a husband who continued to live with such a wife became guilty of her sin. The author of the *"Pastor"* did not indicate the presence of a legal presumption of knowledge of the fact on the part of the husband. Accordingly he did not require that proof of the ignorance of the fact be adduced.[9]

---

strangled and from fornication; from which things keeping yourselves, you shall do well."—the prescriptions of the Council of Jerusalem—circa A.D. 50 (Acts, 15:29).

[7] *De Pudicitia*, c. 1—*MPL*, II, 981—Lohmuller, *The Promulgation of Law*, The Catholic University of America Canon Law Studies, n. 241 (Washington, D. C.: The Catholic University of America Press, 1947), p. 60, footnote n. 6.

[8] Amann, "Penitence," *Dictionnaire de Théologie Catholique* (15 vols. in 30, Paris, 1903-1948), XII, 789; Lohmuller, *op. cit.*, p. 60, footnote 7.

[9] Lib. II, mand. IV, cap. 1: "Et dixi illi: Domine, si quis habuerit uxorem fidelem in Domino, et hanc invenerit in adulterio, numquid peccat vir, si convivat cum illa? Et dixit mihi: Quamdiu nescit peccatum ejus, sine crimine est vir vivens cum illa."—Migne, *Patrologiae Cursus Completus, Series Graeca* (162 vols., Parisiis, 1857-1866), II, 919-920 (hereafter cited *MPG*).

The Penitential Books with their formalistic precision and rigid rules gave but slight consideration to the subjective elements involved in the violation of law. They contain mention of specific mitigated penalties which were to be inflicted on those who violated the law in ignorance. However, the *Ordo Romanus,* under the title *"Ordo Feriae IIII in capite jejunii,"* directed the priest when receiving a penitent to consider his condition, whether he was rich or poor, a mere child or a grown youth, *informed or ignorant.*[10]

An old decree of uncertain date and origin[11] dealt with the distribution of Holy Communion by a heretic to those who were ignorant of the prohibition of the Church and to those who had knowledge of the Church's prohibition to receive Holy Communion from him. Both acts gave rise to penalties; in the former instance there resulted a penance of one year for the material offender after he became aware of the Church's prohibitive law, and in the latter, a penance of ten years. Evidently the offenders were presumed to know the law. If they did not know the law, then those who alleged ignorance of the law were bound to furnish proof for what they alleged, since the penalties were milder for the ignorant than for those who knowingly violated the law.[12]

---

[10] "Non omnibus vero una eademque discertio sit; unicuique eorum, hoc est, inter divitem et pauperem, . . . infantem et puerum . . . scientem et ignarum . . . utrum voluntarie vel casu . . . discernat." This text is taken from the *Codex Manuscript, Valicellanum* D. 5 (tenth century)—H. J. Schmitz, *Die Bussbücher und die Bussdisciplin der Kirche* (2 vols., Mainz, 1883-1898), I, 88; Swoboda, *op. cit.*, p. 18.

[11] The text of this decree was included in the *Decretum Gratiani*—c. 41, C. XXIV, q. 1. E. Friedberg (1837-1910) indicated that two codices ascribed it to Pope Julianus (?); five others attributed it to Pope Lucianus (253-254).—*Corpus Iuris Canonici* (2. ed., 2 vols., Lipsiae: Tauchnitz, 1879-1881), I, 983, note 646. The edition of the *Correctores Romani* (Romae, 1582) attributed it to Pope Julius (337-352). The *Decretum Burchardi* (ca. 1012) ascribed it to Pope Eutychianus (283-296).—*MPL,* CXL, 1004-1005—Swoboda, *op. cit.* p. 19, note 23.

[12] Hinchius, *Das Kirchenrecht der Katholiken und Protestanten in Deutschland* (6 vols. Berlin, 1869-1897), V, 922, note 2 (hereafter cited *Kirchenrecht*); Swoboda, *op. cit.* p. 19, note 24.

2. *The Penitential Practice of the East*

The legal system of the East was concerned almost exclusively with the objective violation of law. The external social order had to be maintained at all costs. With the decline of the Graeco-Roman and Christian culture as occasioned through the barbarian invasions, the absolute character of the law assumed new prominence in Asia Minor. Ignorance of law or of fact was given no consideration, for severe penalties were meted out for the mere material violation of law through ignorance.[13]

St. Basil (329-379) stated that the exercise of all sacred functions was forbidden to a priest who "*insciens illicitis nuptiis implicatus est.*" Ignorance did not excuse him from this law; he was barred from the exercise of his priestly duties, and furthermore was admonished to beg forgiveness for the sin he had committed in ignorance.[14].

In his second canonical epistle St. Basil advised that a woman remain unmarried if she had unknowingly married a man who had already contracted a valid marriage. Ignorance of law did not excuse from invalidating laws. The relationship in this case was described as a "*fornicatio imprudens.*"[15]

3. *Prescriptions of the Penitential Books*

The legal system which grew up in the British Isles and later spread to the Continent differed widely from that of the East. Nevertheless the penitential books considered only the objective or material violations of law. Like the primitive Germanic law, the formalistic system of the British Isles precisely fixed the exact penalty to be imposed every time the external order was disturbed.

The letter of the law had to be followed. The judge or priest was not free to mitigate the legal prescriptions in a particular case.

---

[13] Cf. M. Müller, *Ethik und Recht in der Lehre von der Verantwortlichkeit*, (Regensburg: Joseph Habbel, 1932), pp. 36-42 (hereafter referred to as *Ethik und Recht*).

[14] *Epistola Canonica II*, c. 27, — *MPG*, XXXII, 723.

[15] *Epistola Canonica II*, c. 46: "Quae viro ad tempus ab uxore derelicto insciens nupsit, ac deinde demissa est, quod prior ad ipsum reversa sit, fornicatio quidem est, sed imprudens." *MPG*, XXXII, 730.

The law explicitly provided milder penalties for offenses committed in ignorance.[16]

Willful violations and such infractions of laws as were committed in ignorance were not looked upon as essentially different. "*Qui inscienter peccat, scienter emendet*" was the rule which obtained. One who was suspected of a violation of law received the full penalty unless he could prove that he had not committed the act. Thus in the work of Benedict the Levite, under the title "*Capitularium Karoli Magni et Ludovici Pii,*" mention was made of the law which forbade the purchase of goods from an unknown person unless a third party certified that the owner of the goods was reputable and honest, and consequently that the material, etc., were his own. This recommendation was required with a view to preventing the purchaser from pleading ignorance if later he learned that the goods were stolen. However, when a purchaser who had dispensed with this recommendation discovered that in ignorance he had dealt with a thief, but the rightful owner accused him of stealing his property, he could prove in either of two ways, by oath or by witnesses, his lack of knowledge that the salesman was a thief, and that consequently he was unaware of the fact that the goods were stolen goods. The judge then permitted him to return half the value of the goods to the rightful owner. If he could not find the thief, he had to restore the remaining half.[17]

ARTICLE 3. PAPAL DECREES

Gratian incorporated in his *Decretum* a number of papal decretals dating from the fifth to the seventh century. These bore many resemblances to the imperial decrees of Rome in so far as they emphasized the inviolable character of the canons and laws of the Church.

Thus Pope St. Leo I (440-461) in a letter to the Emperor Marcian (450-457) under date 452 stated that the privileges instituted through the canons of the Holy Church and fixed in the decrees of the venerable Council of Nicaea could not be

[16] Cf. Müller, *Ethik und Recht*, pp. 42-68.

[17] *Capitularium Karoli Magni et Ludovici Pii*, lib. VI, cap. 351—Mansi.

done away with through disapproval, nor could they be changed through innovations.[18]

Pope St. Gregory I (590-604) in 598 commanded that his decrees which were set up in the form of privileges and laws had to be observed in perpetuity and without violation; no bishop could disregard them in whole or in part for any pretext whatsoever. He explained furthermore that it was noxious and inimical to the good character of the priesthood that those things which were ordained should be set aside for the slightest reason (*quantacumque rationis excusatione*).[19]

In the same year Gregory stated that whatever things were done contrary to the law were to be considered both of no effect and invalid: ". . . quae contra leges fiunt non solum inutilia, sed etiam pro infectis habenda sint."[20]

The same pontiff in a letter dated 599 stated the following principle: *"rem quae culpa caret, in damnum vocari non convenit."* This showed some regard for the subjective elements involved in the violation of law. But it would be wrong to deduce too much from the text itself, since Pope Gregory had in mind the *"ignorantes"* who violated a law prior to its promulgation. He said nothing of the ignorance which obtained even after the effective promulgation of the law.[21] Nevertheless this principle had considerable significance even several centuries later, and was frequently cited in the writings then current.

Pope Nicholas I (858-867), in a response to King Charles the Bald (843-877) concerning the abettors of and those who communicated with Engeltrude of Vienne, the excommunicated

---

[18] C. 17, C. XXV, q. 2; Jaffé, *Regesta Pontificum Romanorum ab condita Ecclesia ad annum post Christum natum MCXCVIII* (2. ed., correctam et auctam auspiciis Gulielmi Wattenbach, curaverunt S. Loewenfeld, F. Kaltenbrunner, P. Ewald, 2 tomes in I vol., Lipsiae, 1885-1888), n. 408 (hereafter cited Jaffé).

[19] C. 7, C. XXV, q. 2; Jaffé, n. 1503.

[20] C. 13, C. XXV, q. 2; Jaffé, n. 1724.

[21] *Ex Registro Gregorii I* (IX, 104) Fortunato Episcopo Neapolitano (599)—Jaffé, n. 1629 (ed. P. Ewald)—Comp. I, 2, *de constitutionibus*, I, 1; c. 2, I, *de constitutionibus*, I, 2: ". . . ne detrimentum ante prohibitionem possint ignorantes incurrere, quod eos postmodum dignum est vetitos sustinere."

wife of Count Boso of Flanders,[22] advised Hincmar of Rheims (845-882), who was to execute the rescript, that a distinction should be made in regard to the crimes committed out of necessity or ignorance and the crimes committed with knowledge and deliberation. The ignorant should not be punished hastily, but their ignorance should be examined for a determination whether it was artless (*vera*) or simulated, i.e. willful. Pope Nicholas in drawing this distinction simply repeated the differentiation of ignorance as formulated by St. Augustine in his *De Gratia et Libero Arbitrio.*[23] The pontiff consequently sanctioned the legal presumption of knowledge with reference both to law and fact.

At a Roman Council held under Pope Gregory VII in 1078 it was decided to exempt whole classes of people from the penalties enacted for those who through ignorance associated with excommunicates, and for those who associated with others who themselves had associated with excommunicates. The exempted classes included the women *(uxores),* the children, the slaves, the servants, and the rustics.[24] Although a legal presumption as favoring an ignorance of *fact* was not expressly granted to them, nevertheless a general assumption of ignorance of fact underlies this conciliar decree. The Council likewise did not explicitly grant favor to the presumption of ignorance of law, but the words in the text, "*nimia simplicitate*" and "*non adeo curiales,*" seem to imply that a presumption regarding ignorance of law did militate in favor of these classes.

One of the decisions of the Council of Piacenza under Urban II in 1095 stated that the Orders of those who were ordained by simoniacal prelates, but who were themselves not guilty of simony, were to be sustained, provided that the recipients could prove that they were ignorant of the sinister intent of the ordaining prelate at the time of their elevation to Orders. The ordinations

---

[22] Mansi, XV, 389; c. 102, C. XI, q. 3—Swoboda, *Ignorance in Relation to the Imputability of Delicts*, p. 24, footnote 39.

[23] Cap. III, n. 5—*MPL*, XLIV, 884-885.

[24] ". . . et omnes alios qui non adeo curiales sunt, ut eorum consilio scelera perpetrentur, et illos qui ignoranter excommunicatis communicant, seu illos qui communicant cum eis qui communicant excommunicatis."—Mansi, XX, 505-506; c. 103, C. Xi, q. 3.

of those who knowingly submitted themselves for the reception of Orders to simoniacal prelates were declared *"irritae."* Those who alleged ignorance in the case were held to furnish proof for their statement.[25]

Although some of these decrees were evidently intended to be provisional, their incorporation in the *Decretum Gratiani* indicated that they were considered in the manner of general law, and thus came to serve as the foundation upon which the Decretists constructed a systematic doctrine.[26]

CONCLUSION

When these historical fragments are placed in a relatively logical grouping, several indications become apparent. Law was understood as a rule of action which was prescribed by a lawful superior and which the subject was bound to obey. This concept of emphasizing the force of law seems to have formed the basis for the legal trends as then current. In some instances it even gave rise to the attitude of regarding most of the laws as invalidating or disqualifying in character. This is particularly true as regards the elements which shaped the formalistic penitential system which seemed to be rooted in this concept of law.

Nevertheless, the principles regarding the subjective elements of law were not completely submerged. Even in the law of the penitentials, the violations committed in ignorance were punished with mitigated penalties. The defendant, furthermore, was allowed to prove his alleged ignorance by means of some satisfactory method of proof. The current legal system was concerned not so much about the subject's knowledge of the law, but rather about the fact whether he violated it knowingly or unknowingly.

Throughout this period the distinction between invalidating and disqualifying laws was not explicitly evidenced. Neither was knowledge of the law, of the penalty, of one's own act, or of the presumption. Neither had any explicit legal principle been shaped with reference to the non-notorious act of another, so

---

[25] C. 108, C. I, q. 1; Jaffé, n. 5540.

[26] Cf. Müller, *Ethik und Recht*, pp. 69-71.

that it called either positively for the presumption of knowledge or negatively for the presumption of ignorance regarding such an act.

All such precise legal concepts, norms and principles were to be developed in detail at a later date, yet they had their beginnings, some more noticeably than others, in the jurisprudence of the earlier centuries.

CHAPTER III

From the Time of Gratian Until the Time of the Council of Trent (1545-1563)

The *Decretum Gratiani,* which occasioned important doctrinal developments in almost all of the departments of Canon Law, was obviously the starting point during this period for a further clarification of the juridical elements which touched the question of ignorance both of law and of fact. During this period the fundamental doctrine on ignorance in relation to invalidating and disqualifying laws became entrenched. Furthermore, the canonists and moralists developed not only a system of divisions and definitions for the various kinds of ignorance, but they also proposed principles which shaped the basis for the present day law. The presumption denying ignorance with reference to law and fact as a positive legal concept became progressively more stabilized for a clearer delineation.

Concrete cases and particular canons and decrees were subjected to discussion and commentary. Consequently there resulted not only a multiplicity of definitions and divisions of ignorance, but likewise there emerged certain principles or rules of law relative to ignorance of law and of fact, and relative also to ignorance with reference to invalidating and disqualifying laws.

Article 1. Gratian and the Decretists

The Decretum treated of ignorance in several places.[1] Gratian introduced, as has been seen in Chapter II, a number of texts from St. Augustine[2] as well as a number of pontifical decrees[3].

The development of the canonical doctrine on ignorance may

[1] *Dictum Gratiani* ante D. XXXVIII; *dictum Gratiani* post c. 12, C. I, q. 4; *dictum Gratiani* post c. 2, C. XV, q. 1.

[2] V. gr., c. 4, C. XXII, q. 2; c. 37, C. XXIII, q. 4; c. 1, C. XV, q. 1; C. 5, D. XXXVIII; c. 1, C. I, q. 4.

[3] C. 4, D. XXXVIII; c. 2, D. LXXXII; c. 4, 7, 9, 11, 12, 13, C. XXV, q. 2.

be traced to the revival of Roman Law in the schools, to the consequent adoption of Roman Law principles, and finally to the contributions made by the scholastic theologians. These three factors gave rise to the fundamental principles on ignorance in a manner distinct from the other periods of Canon Law history. The following articles will deal with the pertinent distinctions, division and principles which with relation to the juridical factor of ignorance were evinced during this period.

1. Distinctions of Theological Origin

In his *Ethica* (or *Scito Teipsum*) Abelard (1079-1142) initiated a distinction between *"ignorantia invicibilis"* and *"negligentia."*[4] The scholastic theologians subsequently substituted *"ignorantia vincibilis"* (as opposed to *"invincibilis"*) for *"negligentia"* as occurring in Abelard's distinction.[5] The Decretists borrowed the *"vincibilis-invincibilis"* division from the theologians, and completed a distinction made by Gratian in the *Decretum.* The latter had noted a difference between ignorance which proceeded from infirmity and ignorance which proceeded from the will.[6]

Further distinctions were drawn in rapid succession. The tripartite division of ignorance into *ignoranta invincibilis (invita), simplex (media)* and *affectata* was adopted. *Ignorantia invincibilis* was of the kind that defied conquest in any manner whatsoever.[7] *Ignorantia simplex* was of the type in which one neither proposed

[4] *Ethica*, c. 14—*MPL*, CLXXVIII, 657.

[5] "Est autem ignorantia invincibilis, et ignorantia vincibilis."—Petrus Lombardus, *Libri Quatuor Sententiarum* (2. ed., PP. Collegii S. Bonaventurae, ad Claras Aquas: Typographia Collegii S. Bonaventurae, 1916), lib. II, dist. XXII, cap. 5.

[6] Cf. Rufinus, *Summa Decretorum* (ed. H. Singer, Paderborn, 1902), p. 345, ad Grat. Dict., c. 1, C. XV, q. 1, s.v. *Quod autem ea, qua mente alienata fiunt.*—Kuttner, *Kanonistische Schuldlehre von Gratian bis auf die Dekretalen Gregors IX*, Studi e Testi, n. 64 (Città del Vaticano: Biblioteca Apostolica Vaticana, 1935), p. 139, note 4 (hereafter cited *Schuldlehre*).

[7] Stephanus Tornacensis, *Summa* (ed. J. F. Schulte, Giessen, 1891), p. 57, ad pr., D. XXXVIII: ". . . ut quando quis laborat, ut sciat, sed . . . proficere non potest . . ."—Kuttner, *Schuldlehre*, p. 141.

nor declined to seek information.[8] *Ignorantia affectata* was such in character when one who was capable of acquiring knowledge nevertheless passed by and spurned all offered opportunity for gaining it.[9].

The Decretists, moreover, distinguished between *"ignorantia poena"* and *"ignorantia culpa"*; the former was an affliction of or deficiency in the mind by which it was hindered from acquiring the requisite knowledge,[10] while the latter pointed to an act of neglect, of contempt, or even of a positive desire to remain ignorant about what one was under necessity of knowing or doing.[11]

Rolandus Bandinelli (d. 1181), borrowing a Roman Law distinction,[12] differentiated between vincible ignorance characterized on the one hand as crass or supine and characterized on the other hand as taxing the effort of even a very discriminating person in its conquest.[13]

2. *Principles of Roman Law Origin*

Gratian formally introduced into the *Decretum* a Roman Law distinction which proved to be of greatest importance to subsequent develpments in canonical doctrines. He divided ignorance on the

[8] Stephanus Tornacensis, *Summa*, p. 57 ad pr. XXXVIII: ". . . ut quando nec appetit nec fugit discere." Cf. Swoboda, *Ignorance in Relation to the Imputability of Delicts*, p. 33, note 16.

[9] Stephanus Tornacensis, *Summa*, *loc. cit:* "Affectata, ut quando potest discere, sed neglegit et contemnit . . ."—Kuttner, *Schuldlehre*, p. 142, note 4.

[10] Huguccio ad pr., D. XXXVIII: ". . . ignorantia poena est animi passio vel defectus quo animus impeditur ad comprehendum vel intelligendum ea quae sunt necessaria . . ."—Kuttner, *Schuldlehre*, p. 144, note 1. Cf. Lottin, "Le problème de l'*ignorantia iuris* de Gratien à St. Thomas d' Aquin"—*Recherches de Théologie ancienne et médiévale*, V (1933), 349-350—Swoboda, *op. cit.*, p. 34, note 20.

[11] Huguccio, *loc cit.*: ". . . ignorantia culpa est negligentia, vel contemptus, qua vel quo quis neglegit vel contemnit scire ea quae debet scire vel facere, vel voluntas qua quaerit ignorare ea . . ."—Kuttner, *Schuldlehre*, p. 144, note 1.

[12] Kuttner, *Schuldlehre*, p. 145.

[13] ". . . item vincibilis . . . quandoque est resupina et crassa; quandoque est talis quae caderet in discretissimum virum."—*Sententiae*, p. 125—Kuttner, *Schuldlehre*, p. 145, note 2.

basis of the unknown object into ignorance of law and ignorance of fact.[14] These two forms of ignorance will accordingly have to be considered separately.

A. Ignorance of fact

The author of the *Decretum* drew a distinction in regard to the objective obligation of knowing the fact.[15] He differentiated between a fact which one ought to know and a fact which one is not obliged to have knowledge of.[16] This distinction disappeared in the later Decretalists.

The decretists, taking the Roman Law "ignorance of law" and "ignorance of fact" division, subdivided *"ignorantia facti quod oportet scire"* into crass or supine ignorance, and into ignorance which for its conquest taxes the effort of even a very discriminating person.[17] The Decretists often cited the example of crass ignorance as given in the *Digest,* namely, not to know what everyone in the city knew.[18]

The *"ignorantia quae caderet in discretissimum virum"* was frequently called *"probabilis,"*[19] and was admitted as at least a presumptively excusing factor in regard to facts pertaining both to others and to oneself.[20] Public facts were presumed to be

---

[14] *Dictum Gratiani,* ad c. 1, C. I, q. 4—"Est enim ignorantia alia facti, alia iuris."

[15] *Dictum Gratiani,* pars IV, § 1, ad c. 12, C. I, q. 4.

[16] *Loc. cit.:* "Facti alia, quod non oportuit eum scire, alia, quod oportuit eum scire."

[17] Stephanus Tornacensis, *Summa,* p. 152, ad *Gratiani Dictum* post c. 12, C. I, q. 4; Simon de Bisiniano, *Summa Decreti,* ad c. 6, C. XXXIV, q. 1-2, — Kuttner, *Schuldlehre,* p. 155, note 1.

[18] ". . . quid enim si omnes in civitate sciant, quod ille solus ignorat?" —D. (22, 6) (9, 2); cf. *Glossa Ordinaria,* ad pr., D. XXXVIII, s. v. *cum itaque.*

[19] *Glossa Ordinaria* ad *Gratiani Dictum* post c. 12, C. 1, q. 4, s. v. *omnis ignorantia.*

[20] *Loc. cit.:* "Ignorantia facti semper excusat sive ignorat de alieno facto, sive de propriis, dum tamen probabilis sit . . . magis tamen excusat error in alieno facto quam proprio, quia probabilis est ignorantia in alieno facto."

known by all.[21] But one could bring proof of the contrary either by way of oath or by showing that one was in another province.[22]

If someone unknowingly was ordained by a simoniacal prelate, his ordination was sustained, provided he himself did not seek ordination through simony. The cleric who pleaded ignorance had to establish its presence with proof. Ioannes Teutonicus (d. 1245) mentioned three ways by which ignorance might be proved, namely, by proving some fact from which it *directly, necessarily,* or *most likely follows that the person was ignorant.*[23]

B. Ignorance of law

The decretists showed a remarkable dependence upon Roman Law and upon the Roman Law glossators in their treatment of law. Gratian himself taught that ignorance of the natural law was not to be condoned in adults.[24] The decretists described an adult as one who is *"discretus"*[25] or as a person who is *"doli capax."*[26] With reference to the mentally weak, and sometimes also with regard to children, the presence of ignorance regarding the natural

[21] *Glossa* ad c. 14, D. XVI, s. v. *regionibus:* ". . . nulli licet ignorare ea quae publice facta sunt."

[22] *Glossa* ad. c. 24, C. XII, q. 2, s. v. *ignorare:* ". . . Sed qualiter probabit se ignorasse? Respondeo, probabit quod fuit in alia provincia, vel etiam proprio iuramento." *Glossa* ad c. 6, C. XXXVIII, q. 1, s. v. *per securitatem:* ". . . id est, iuramentum . . . testes enim habere non possunt de huiusmodi, et sic patet quod per iuramentum probatur ignorantia." The latter text related to a man who unknowingly had carnal relations with his sister-in-law.

[23] *Glossa Ordinaria,* ad c. 108, C. I, q. 1, s. v. *probare:* ". . . qui ignorantiam allegat, eam probare debet . . . probatio tripliciter fiat . . . *directe* cum probato eo, ex quo id quod intendit *necessario* aut *verisimiliter* sequitur: ignorantiae tunc verisimilis probatio sufficit."

[24] *Dictum Gratiani,* pars IV, §1, ad c. 12, C. I, q. 4: "Naturalis (ignorantia) omnibus adultis damnabilis est."

[25] ". . . si est adultus vel discretus . . ."—*Glossa Ordinaria* ad pr., D. XXXVIII.

[26] *Summa Bambergensis,* ad *Gratiani Dictum* post c. 12, C. I, q. 4—Kuttner, *Schuldlehre,* p. 165.

law could be condoned.[27] However, these exceptions were not universally admitted.[28]

Gratian stated that ignorance of the civil law was excusable in minors.[29] A person was judged a minor in accordance with the Roman Law norms, i.e., when he was below twenty-five years of age.[30]

The decretists, invoking a further distinction which was based on the consideration of one's status in society, left room for ignorance both of civil and of canon law[31] to become an excusing factor for minors,[32] for women, for soldiers and for rustics.[33] However, ignorance of law as a possible excusing factor was expressly disclaimed for clerics;[34] their possession of knowledge had necessarily to be presumed in view of the high office they held.

Ioannes Teutonicus (d. 1245), when commenting on c. 2, D. LXXXII, indicated some applicable norms in relation to those who pleaded ignorance of law. Upon the public act of promulgation of a law, everyone was duty-bound to have knowledge

---

[27] Lottin, "Le problème de l'*ignorantia iuris* de Gratien à St. Thomas d'Aquin," *Recherches de Théologie ancienne et médiévale*, V (1933), 345-368.

[28] "Damasus (*Add. ad Glos. Ord. Tancredi* ad c. 3, Comp. I, *de apostatis et reiterantibus baptisma*, V. 9): ". . . immo iura canonica loquencia de receptione baptismi quasi naturalia sunt, quia modificant ius naturale . . . unde nec aetas nec rusticitas per ignorantiam excusatur in eo."—Kuttner, *Schuldlehre*, p. 170, note 3.

[29] *Dictum*, Pars IV, § 2, post c. 12, C. I, q. 4.

[30] Paucapalea, *Summa Paucapalea* (ed. J. F. Schulte [Giessen, 1890], p. 55) ad c. 12, C. I, q. 4; C. (1, 18) 2.

[31] *Glossa Ordinaria*, ad *Dictum Gratiani cit.*, c. 12, C. I, q. 4; cf. Kuttner, *Schuldlehre*, p. 164, note 4.

[32] Paucapalea, *Summa*, *loc. cit.*

[33] "Ignorantia iuris civilis vel canonici . . . aliquos . . . excusat, ut milites, mulieres, rusticos, minores."—*Glossa Ordinaria* (Ioannes Teutonicus) ad pr., D. XXXVIII. Stephanus Tornacensis (*Summa*, ad *Dictum Gratiani* post c. 12, C. 1, q. 4, s. v. *aliis permittitur*—ed. Schulte, p. 153): "Ut pupillo ob beneficium aetatis, et militibus, qui propter rempublicam occupantur in castris . . . et rusticis propter commodum agriculturae, et quandoque mulieribus propter sexum."—Swoboda, *Ignorance in Relation to the Imputability of Delicts*, p. 38.

[34] Cf. Kuttner, *Schuldlehre*, p. 168, note 2.

of the law.[35] The presumption of knowledge was thus sufficiently established, so that anyone who nevertheless pleaded ignorance had to furnish proof of his alleged lack of knowledge.[36]

Anyone who rightfully pleaded ignorance could in substantiation of his claim take an oath *(sacramentum);* or the person was perhaps able to show that he was elsewhere at the time of promulgation; or perhaps the chapter *(collegium vel aliquis conventus)* could under oath testify regarding his ignorance, and thus sufficient proof could avail. In this case *("Proposuisti")* the bishop and the major members of the chapter were required to take the oath.[37]

ARTICLE 2. FROM THE DECRETALS OF GREGORY IX TO THE COUNCIL OF TRENT

The Decretals of Gregory IX (1234) and the commentaries written on this official collection repeated the doctrines and principles as enunciated in Gratian and by the commentators on the *Decretum.* This period likewise furnished a greater degree of uniformity and continuity in respect to distinctions and principles, and furthermore witnessed the presentation of new and important doctrine regarding the factor of ignorance in relation to invalidating laws.

1. The Decretal "Ad Apostolicam"[38]

This Decretal of Pope Innocent III (1198-1216) marked the Church's point of departure from the rule of Roman Law, *"Quae contra ius fiunt, debent utique pro infectis haberi."*[39] The Pontiff was asked whether one was to be regarded as validly professed if his profession had been made before the year's probation was

[35] ". . . Sum enim constitutio sit publice promulgata, quilibet eam tenetur scire . . . secundum leges tenetur eam quilibet scire usque ad duos menses."—*Glossa Ordinaria,* ad c. 2, D. LXXXII, s. v. *non probatur.*

[36] ". . . tenebantur ipsi probare ignorantiam . . ."—*Glossa Ordinaria,* ad c. 2, D. LXXXII.

[37] ". . . sufficit si episcopus cum maioribus de capitulo iurat."—*Glossa Ordinaria,* ad c. 2, D. LXXXII.

[38] C. 16, X, *de regularibus et transeuntibus ad religionem,* III, 31.

[39] C. (1, 14) 5; cf. also Reg. 64, R. J., in VI°.

completed. The Pope replied that such a profession was valid, provided the monk had received the habit and the abbot had accepted the profession; for many things, though they were forbidden, were nevertheless valid when done.[40]

This rule applied to those laws which did not contain a perpertual prohibition,[41] that is, to all laws which did not contain an invalidating clause.[42] Ioannes Andreae (1272-1348), in his gloss on the sixty-fourth *Regula Iuris: "Quae contra ius fiunt, debent utique pro infectis haberi,"* observed that this rule of law applied to those cases which were governed by a perpetual prohibition.[43] With regard to the things which, though done contrary to law, were nevertheless regarded as valid, Ioannes Andreae remarked: "*. . . illa non sunt directe contra ius: quia, licet ius non assistat, non tamen plene resistit.*" If the lawmaker intended that contrary acts be regarded as invalid, he explicitly made mention of this[44].

2. *Ignorance of Fact*

During the period of the decretalists greater emphasis was placed upon the distinction between the *ignorantia probabilis* and the *ignorantia crassa*. Those who pleaded *ignorantia probabilis* were confronted with the task of establishing by means of proof the fact of its presence. Thus the postulation and election of an

---

[40] ". . . quia multa fieri prohibentur, quae, si facta fuerint, obtinent roboris firmitatem."—c. 16, X, *de regularibus et transeuntibus ad religionem,* III, 31.

[41] *Glossa* ad c. 16, X, *de regularibus, etc.,* III, 31, s. v. *casus:* "Haec regula locum habet in his quae non habent perpetuam prohibitionem . . ."

[42] *Glossa* ad *loc cit.:* ". . . quia non cavetur in prohibitione quod si factum fuerit, non valebit." Panormitanus, *Commentaria in Quinque Libros Decretalium* (5 vols. in 7, Venetiis, 1588), lib. III, 31, cap. 16, n. 11: ". . . ubi legis prohibitio non habet perpetuam causam prohibitionis, actus in contrarium gestus non annullatur. Prohibitio autem de qua hic temporalis." Hereafter this work of Panormitanus will be cited as *Commentaria.*

[43] *Glossa* ad Reg. 64, R. J., in VI°: ". . . in iis quae perpetuam habent prohibitionis causam."

[44] *Glossa* ad hunc locum: "addit, quod si contra prohibitionem fiat, non valeat."

illegitimate person was in law ruled to be null and void. Furthermore, the electors were automatically deprived of their power of electing unless they could prove that they were ignorant of the illegitimacy of the candidate. Accordingly, in vindication of their electoral right, they had first to furnish proof that they had made a diligent search into the personal background and character of the one elected. In accordance with the allowable usage and practice then current, proof of the existing *ignorantia probabilis* could be established by means of an oath.[45]

A refusal to take the oath was considered an admission of crass ignorance,[46] whereas he who took the oath could prevail against the *"praesumptio iuris"* that he was in possession of knowledge.[47] The law generally presumed that the agent knew what he was doing,[48] and hence those who alleged ignorance had to furnish proof in substantiation of their claim.[49] Hostiensis (d. 1271) observed that in occult matters one could very readily plead ignorance.[50] But this was not true in regard to public facts; everyone was presumed to have knowledge of what everyone else knew.[51]

Ioannes Andreae repeated the same doctrine in his gloss to

---

[45] *Glossa* ad c. 20, X, *de electione et electi potestate*, I, 6, s. v. *ignorantiam:* ". . . crassa fuit istorum ignorantia qua improvide ipsum elegerunt, non requirentes de eius persona ab his per quos certificari potuerunt, et ideo debebant probare diligentiam adhibitam: at sic probarent ignorantiam; hanc ignorantiam poterant probare per iuramentum."

[46] Cf. c. 4, X, *de sententia excommunicationis*, V, 39.

[47] *Glossa* ad c. 6, X, *qui matrimonium accusare possunt, vel contra illud testari*, IV, 18, s. v. *iuramento:* ". . . nota hic quod plus valet iuramentum unius quam praesumptio iuris: quia per istud iuramentum eliditur iuris praesumptio."

[48] Cf. c. 20, X, *de electione et electi potestate*, I, 6: ". . . nec probare cogimus ignorantiam quam allegant."

[49] *Glossa* ad hunc locum: ". . . unde probare debebant isti ignorantiam quam allegabant."

[50] *Commentaria in Quinque Decretalium Libros* (5 vols. in 3, Venetiis, 1581), ad c. 1, X, *de postulatione praelatorum*, I, 5, lib. I, tit. 4, c. 1, n. 21: "In occultis autem bene potest ignorantia allegari." (This work is hereafter cited *Commentaria*).

[51] Hostiensis, *Commentaria*, ad c. 13, X, *de electione et electi potestate*, I, 6, lib. I, cap. 13, n. 13.

Boniface VIII's forty-seventh *Regula Juris: "Praesumitur ignorantia, ubi scientia non probatur."* He stated:

> ". . . circa ea quae publice fiunt, *praesumitur scientia,* nisi probetur ignorantia: circa ea autem quae fiunt occulte, praesumitur ignorantia, nisi probetur scientia, ut hic. Et scias quod haec regula vera est in his quae quis scire vel indagare non tenetur."[52]

Furthermore, he pointed out three ways by means of which alleged ignorance might be proved: first, by oath; secondly, by proving some fact from which it necessarily followed that the person was ignorant, e. g., by proving the insanity of the agent; and, thirdly, by proving a fact from which it followed in all probability, though not with absolute necessity, that the person was ignorant, e. g., by proving that the person was not present at a given time.[53]

If, without obtaining the needed permission, a bishop ordained someone who was not his subject, it was presumed that he proceeded knowingly in defiance of the law, and consequently he was liable to suspension for one year, unless he could prove that he was ignorant;[54] an oath in attestation of his ignorance proved sufficient to nullify the presumption that he had knowledge of the fact.[55] A bishop who through affected ignorance presumed to ordain a non-subject was under the same penalty; his affected ignorance was juridically deemed the equivalent of knowledge.[56] If he pleaded ignorance by way of oath, his accusers necessarily had to prove through arguments or probable conjectures that he had knowledge or that he acted in affected ignorance.[57]

---

[52] *Glossa* ad Reg. 47, R. J., in VI°.

[53] *Loc. cit.*

[54] *Glossa* ad c. 2, *de temporibus ordinationum et qualitate ordinandorum,* I, 9, in VI°, s. v. *scienter:* . . ."quod praesumitur sciens, nisi probet ignorantiam."

[55] *Glossa* ad hunc locum: ". . . videtur autem ad eam probandam sufficiere iuramentum."

[56] *Glossa* ad hunc locum, s. v. *affectata:* "Aequipollent ergo scientia et affectata ignorantia."

[57] *Glossa* ad *loc. cit.,* s. v. *affectata:* ". . . si iuravit se ignorare . . . altera pars habebit necesse probare scientiam vel affectatam ignorantiam: et probabitur hoc per argumenta, vel coniecturas probabiles."

3. Ignorance of Law

During the decretal and post-decretal period the strict legislation regarding ignorance of law continued. The decretalists repeated the rigid and traditional doctrines of the decretists. Nevertheless the existence of ignorance of law was generally conceded to be possible and even probable among certain classes of people; however, the *natural law* made no allowance for a presumption of ignorance in favor of anyone.[58]

Ioannes Andreae, when commenting on the *Regula Juris:* "Praesumitur ignorantia, ubi scientia non probatur,"[59] remarked that this rule of law did not apply in relation to ignorance of the natural law.[60] Consequently the possession of knowledge regarding the natural law was presumed. The same general presumption of knowledge applied in relation to evangelical truths, articles of faith and the sacraments.[61]

A constitution of Pope Boniface VIII[62] implied that the *statutes of ordinaries* did not rest as an obligation upon those who were in *ignorantia probabilis* regarding such statutes, for it stated that those who were ignorant about the statutes were not bound by them as long as their ignorance was not crass or supine.[63] This decretal, then, touched simply the question of ignorance with

---

[58] Hostiensis, *Commentaria*, c. 4, X, *de eo qui duxit in matrimonium quam polluit*, IV, 8, n. 2: ". . . licet enim feminis liceat allegare . . . ignorantiam iuris . . . non tamen . . . ignorantia evangelicae veritatis . . . nec ignorantia iuris naturalis probabilis est."

[59] Reg. 47, R. J., in VI°.

[60] *Loc cit.:* ". . . notandum . . . quia ignorantia iuris praecipue naturalis non excusat . . . de tali ignorantia non loquitur haec regula."

[61] Cf. Hostiensis, *Commentaria, loc. cit.*; also Henricus Boich (d. ca. 1350), *In Quinque Decretalium Libros Commentaria* (Venetiis, 1576), c. 1, X, *de delictis puerorum*, V. 23: ". . . illud tamen non habet locum in articulis fidei, vel sacramentis . . ."

[62] C. 2, *de constitutionibus*, I, 2, in VI°.

[63] *Loc. cit.:* "Ut animarum periculis obvietur, sententiis per statuta quorumcumque ordinariorum prolatis ligari nolumus ignorantes: dum tamen eorum ignorantia crassa non fuerit aut supina"; ". . . statuta ordinariorum non ligant probabiliter ignorantes."—inscriptio ad hoc caput.

reference to particular statutes. Its rule was not meant to be applicable with reference to universal legislation as well.[64]

The early commentators on the decretal law regarded this constitution as containing an exception to the general rule, "Ignorantia facti, non iuris, excusat."[65] They interpreted it strictly, and consequently they did not consider it as applicable also to the question of ignorance regarding the general law, i. e., the decrees of the Pontiffs.[66]

The commentators on the Gregorian decretals adopted and developed some of the decretists' opinions relative to the effect which the promulgation of a law exercised on the factor of ignorance regarding that law. Some of the decretists had distinguished between ignorance of law as existing after the passage of a law *(conditio)* but before its promulgation, and ignorance as obtaining only after the promulgation of the law. They taught that prior to the proper publication of a law all ignorance regarding the law should be regarded as ignorance of fact, while after the publication all continued ignorance became ignorance of law. Thus the actual intervening promulgation of the law served to characterize the existing ignorance either as ignorance of law or as ignorance of fact.[67] In line with the nature of the law in question, the law was presumed to be known by all alike, either at the very time of the promulgation itself, or within two months thereafter.[68] But the one who alleged ignorance could render the legal presumption of knowledge nugatory if he proved that it was impossible for him to have knowledge of the law.[69] This he could accomplish by showing through documents or witnesses

---

[64] *Glossa* ad hunc loc., s. v. *statuta:* "De generalibus ergo statutis canonum non loquitur, quae ab omnibus sciri et custodiri debent."

[65] D. (22, 6) 9, pr; Reg. 13, R. J., in VI°.

[66] Cf. Boich, *Commentaria*, c. 2, de constitutionibus, I, 2, in VI°.

[67] Cf. Kuttner, *Schuldlehre*, pp. 173-175. This was the opinion of the *Summa Monacensis*, of Huguccio and of Ioannes Teutonicus.—*Op. cit.*, p. 174, note 1. Cf. also Swoboda, *Ignorance in Relation to the Imputability of Delicts*, p. 51, note 97.

[68] Cf. *Glossa Ordinaria*, ad c. 2, X, *de constitutionibus*, I, 2; Hostiensis, *Commentaria*, ad c. 2, X, *de constitutionibus*, I, 2.

[69] Hostiensis, *Commentaria*, ad c. 2, X, *de constitutionibus*, I, 2: ". . . nisi forte dilucide probaret suam ignorantiam."

that he was insane at the time, that as a ward he was not answerable to the law, that he was confined in prison, that he was relegated to an island, or that he was cut off from contact with human society.[70] Thus he could establish the character of his ignorance as *probabilis*. With reference to the promulgation of a particular statute one could prove his ignorance by showing that he was not in the territory when the law was promulgated.[71]

A final point remains to be considered under *ignorance of law*. There are several interesting cases which reflect the development of the specific doctrine regarding *ignorance of invalidating laws*. The formation of this doctrine derived principally from several decretals contained in the *Liber Sextus*.

C. 1, *de concessione praebendae et ecclesiae non vacantis*, III, 7, in VI°, described a case in which a mandate had been given to a certain person in assurance of his appointment to a particular benefice when it would become vacant; however, when the vacancy occurred the ordinary conferred the benefice on another, who accepted the dignity connected with the benefice. At the moment the benefice was accepted, the decree of conferment became effective, and even though the person who was first promised the benefice was ignorant of the acceptation by the second party, he could exercise no claim to the dignity.[72]

Another decretal[73] treated of a papal legate who by apostolic authority had the power of accepting resignations from benefices

---

[70] Boich, *Commentaria*, ad c. 2, X, *de constitutionibus*, I, 2: ". . . quod intelligo si probaret per testes vel aliqua documenta se tempore dictae constitutionis fuisse furiosum vel mente captum vel pupillum non doli capacem . . . per illud tempus stetisset in carcere clauso vel in heremo vel insula inhabitabili."

[71] *Glossa Ordinaria*, ad c. 2, X *de constitutionibus*, I, 2, s. v. *ante prohibitionem*.

[72] *Glossa Ordinaria* ad hunc locum, s. v. *referri:* ". . . Papa enim non vult quod statim assumat illud decretum suum vigorem: sed tunc cum acceptaverit, valet: etiam si ille, ad quem pertinet collatio, ignoraverit acceptationem: quia decretum sumit vigorem, et ligat ignorantes." Also *ibid.*, s. v. *esset:* ". . . licet hoc non ignoret: non tamen ignorabat collationem per Priorem factam ante vacationem et acceptationem non valere: et ideo istae allegationes ignorantiae parum prosunt."

[73] C. 14, *de praebendis et dignitatibus*, III, 4, in VI°.

and of conferring these benefices on others. If the Supreme Pontiff, without making mention of the power which he had granted to the legate, conferred on someone a particular benefice which was under the jurisdiction of the legate, and thereupon the legate, *ignorant of the Pope's action,* conferred it upon another, the conferment made by the Pope stood firm; the subsequent act of the delegate did not achieve any juridical effect.[74]

A third decretal[75] settled a doubt regarding the conferment of the same benefice by Popes Nicholas IV (1288-1292) and Celestine V (1294). Pope Nicholas promised the conferment of a certain benefice when it later became vacant. His successor promised the same benefice, still not vacant, to a second party, and specified that the latter was to be preferred before all others, even to those who by apostolic or any other authority might have received a previous mandate. However, when the benefice became vacant it was actually conferred upon the incumbent named by Nicholas. This incumbent was unaware of the fact that Pope Celestine had ever promised the benefice to anyone else. Pope Boniface VIII (1294-1303), who succeeded Celestine, settled the question; he decreed that the actual granting of the benefice to the first incumbent was invalid since the conferment was made after and contrary to the decree of Celestine. This held even though the one who conferred the benefice, or also the one who received it, was ignorant of the later papal decree. Consequently, ignorance did not excuse from invalidity. The Pontiff stated: "Prima enim collatio, post et contra decretum a dicto Coelestino interpositum facta, licet ab ignorantibus et etiam ignoranti, non obtinet firmitatem."[76]

Another case[77] was that which touched the election and confirmation in office of a certain Sclata who had been elected as

---

[74] *Glossa Ordinaria* ad hunc locum, s. v. *casus:* ". . . decretum irritans in reservatione ligat ignorantes . . . nec est necessarium quod gratia cum decreto notificetur collatori: sed absque aliqua notificatione manus ordinarii sunt adeo ligatae, quod beneficium vacans non potest alii conferre."

[75] C. 40, X, *de praebendis et dignitatibus,* III, 4, in VI°.

[76] *Loc. cit.*

[77] C. 45, X, *de electione et electi potestate,* I, 6, in VI°.

the archbishop of Bologna. Two days after the death of Octavianus, the canons of the archdiocese, fearing that the Pope would reserve the archbishopric, chose Sclata as his successor. As was anticipated, Boniface on hearing of the death of Octavianus did reserve the appointment to the Holy See, and furthermore decreed that the canons should not choose a successor. Three days later the Pope learned of the election of Sclata. This election proved altogether acceptable to the Pontiff. Since the election had preceded his act of reservation, Pope Boniface honored the election as valid, but his decree of reservation did affect all the subsequent acts, and therefore made them devoid of juridical effect. The act of confirmation in office accordingly pertained exclusively to the Roman Pontiff. All acts contrary to the conditions as incorporated in the act of papal reservation were therefore of no effect. This consequence obtained whether it was consciously or in ignorance that anyone had undertaken the performance of any acts that contravened the papal reservation.[78]

These decretals were appealed to frequently by the commentators. They demonstrated that papal enactments, if they carried the threat of invalidity for acts performed to the contrary, were binding on all alike, the ignorant as well as the informed. The commentators of the following period used these decretals as the basis for the canonical contributions which they make in this regard.

---

[78] *Loc. cit.:* "... decernentes, si secus super hoc a quoquam scienter vel ignoranter attentum exstiterit, irritum et inane."

CHAPTER IV

From the Time of the Council of Trent Until the Code of Canon Law (1918)

General Characteristics

Relative to the matter here considered, the post-Tridentine period is not characterized by any positive legislation on the part of the Church. The canonists and moralists during this period were responsible for the further developments that occurred with reference to the doctrine respecting ignorance in its various phases. The norms which they established were founded upon their moral and legal reasoning, and the binding force which these norms obtained was brought about through custom.[1]

Particularly noticeable during this period is the fact that the juridical factor of ignorance received treatment not simply as occasion presented itself, but the doctrines regarding it were collected together and discussed according to the scholastic method of definition, division and statement of principles.[2]

The definition and divisions of ignorance remained substantially unchanged during this period. However, the term *"probabilis"* was frequently supplanted by the theological terms: *"invincibilis,*

---

[1] Cf. Hinschius, *Kirchenrecht*, V, 923-924.

[2] V. gr., Covarrubias y Leyva, *In Bonifacii VIII Constitutionem quae incipit, Alma Mater, Commentarii* (*Opera Omni*, 2 vols., Coloniae Allobrogum, 1679), Pars I, X; Sanchez, *De Sancto Matrimonii Sacramento* (3 vols in 2, Antverpiae, 1607), lib. IX, disp. XXXII (hereafter cited *De Matrimonio*); Alterius, *De Censuris Ecclesiasticis* (Romae, 1618), lib. III, disp. II, cap. III; Passerinus, *Commentaria in Sextum Librum Decretalium* (Venetiis, 1698) lib. I, tit. II, cap. II, q. 1 (hereafter cited *Commentaria*); Pirhing, *Ius Canonicum Nova Methodo Explicatum* (5 vols. in 4, Dilingae, 1674-1678), lib. V, tit. XXXIX, sect. II, nn. 42-46 (hereafter cited *Ius Canonicum*); Saurez, *De Censuris*, disp. IV, sect. VIII-XI—*Opera Omnia* (26 vols., Parisiis, 1856-1861), XXIII, pp. 127-139.

involuntaria or *inculpabilis,*" and the terms "*vincibilis, voluntaria* or *culpabilis*" were substituted for the term "crassa." It was in this manner that the former "*probabilis-crassa*" distinction, as initiated by the canonists, was given a new adaptation and expression by the moralists.[3]

During this period the concept of affected ignorance acquired a more precise meaning in that it was accepted as referring to ignorance which was directly procured for the express purpose of eluding the obligation of the law. The meaning of crass ignorance likewise became more clarified in that it was accepted as denoting ignorance which, though it was but indirectly willed, nevertheless resulted from negligence of a particularly remiss degree. This distinction was taken into Canon Law literature[4] from the distinction which St. Thomas (1225-1274) had made between "*ignorantia directa et per se voluntaria*" and "*ignorantia indirecta et per accidens voluntaria.*"[5] The ultimate distinction, the one between *ignorantia voluntaria*" and "*ignorantia involuntaria*" as then understood, was a contribution made by Alexander of Hales (ca. 1165-1245).[6]

Finally, attention should also be called to the distinction between ignorance of law and ignorance of fact. In many instances both forms of ignorance were in their juridical implications judged according to the same standard, namely the amount of diligence that one had to exercise in order to acquire the necessary knowledge. The authors recognized the obligation of acquiring the knowledge which one needed to have in view of one's state in life or by reason of one's office, but they also admitted that at times a person could without fault lack knowledge of matters

[3] Cf. Navarrus, *Consiliorum sive Responsorum Libri Quinque* (*Romae*, 1602), Pars. I, lib. I, *de constitutionibus*, cons. I, n. 2.

[4] V. gr., Gonzalez-Tellez, *Commentaria Perpetua in Singulos Textus Quinque Librorum Decretalium Gregorii IX* (5 vols. in 4, Lugduni, 1715), lib. V, tit. XXVII, c. 9, n. 1 (hereafter cited *Commentaria Perpetua*); Passerinus, *Commentaria*, lib. I, tit. II, cap. II, q. 1, art. 5-6.

[5] *Summa Theologica*, Ia IIae, q. 76, art. 4.

[6] *Summa Theologica* (3 vols., ed. PP. Collegii S. Bonaventurae, ad Claras Aquas: Typographia Collegii S. Bonaventurae, 1924-1930), lib. II, pars II, inq. III, tract. II, sect. I, q. II, tit. I, cap. 8.

that pertained to his office or station. In like manner, although it was to be presumed that one had knowledge of what was known in general to everyone else, yet one's knowledge could suffer loss through forgetfulness or for other equivalent reasons.[7]

ARTICLE 1. IGNORANCE OF LAW

In the forum of conscience one could plead ignorance as an excuse whenever the ignorance was invincible, amenable to condonation *(probabilis),* or free from moral deficiency. Proof of these factors was not required. However, when such ignorance was pleaded in a judicial tribunal, then its existence had to become established through proof. Furthermore, the right to allege ignorance and error was restricted within the realm of only such ignorance and error as could be established through proof.[8]

In the period between the Council of Trent and the promulgation of the present Code of Canon Law the authors continued to expound the traditional rules, principles and doctrines in regard to the juridical consequences flowing from ignorance and error. They repeated the rule that ignorance and error with reference to the law are not presumed.[9]

This *praesumptio iuris,* so thoroughly and completely vindicated through the centuries, presupposed that the law itself, being a regulation in according with reason, had been promulgated by the head of the community for the sake of the common welfare.[10] Laws had to be officially proposed to the community as a guiding rule of action. Through promulgation they became "*publica*" or

---

[7] Suarez, *De Censuris,* disp. IV, sect. VIII, n. 12-19—*Opera Omnia,* XXIII, pp. 130-132.

[8] Passerinus, *Commentaria,* lib. I, cap. II, ques. I, art. XXV, n. 494.

[9] Passerinus, *Commentaria,* lib. I, tit. II, cap. II, q. I, art. 25, n. 472; Mascardus, *De Probationibus* (3 vols., Venetiis, 1593-1595), Vol. I, concl. 78, n. 7; Suarez, *De Censuris,* disp. 4, sect. 8, n. 19—*Opera Omnia,* XXIII, pp. 129-132; Reiffenstuel, *Jus Canonicum Universum* (7 vols., Parisiis, 1864-1870), ad Reg. 13, R.J., in VI°.

[10] Cf. the definition of law by St. Thomas Aquinas in his *Summa Theologica,* Ia IIae, q. 90, art. 4.

"notoria."[11] Previous to promulgation they lacked binding force.[12] Not until promulgation had taken place were laws presumed to be known, and reciprocally ignorance was not presumed after the act of promulgation.

The same presumption held in the following instances: when the law was universally known or known by the majority; when it had been observed commonly for a long time; and when the law had been incorporated in particular or in general legislation. In all these cases excusable ignorance was not presumed, so that those who lacked knowledge of the law were presumed to be in supine or crass ignorance.[13] Those who were in error regarding a *"ius civile notorium vel indubitatum"* were presumed to be guilty of *"dolus."*[14] In some cases the presumption of knowledge of the law was so strong that one was not regarded capable of alleging ignorance. Thus no one could plead ignorance of papal decrees which after their initial publication had subsequently become clarified or explained. Only in such instances in which no declaratory statements had as yet emanated from the Holy See could anyone hope to be sustained in his plea of ignorance regarding the papal law.[15]

Ignorance of the *natural law* could not be pleaded as an excuse;[16]

---

[11] Passerinus, *Commentaria*, lib. I, tit. II, q. I, art. 25, n. 477.

[12] Prosper Fagnanus, *Commentaria in Quinque Libros Decretalium* (4 vols., Romae, 1661), lib. I, tit. *de constitutionibus*, cap. XIII, n. 42 (hereafter cited *Commentaria*)—". . . tria requiri ad esse legis, primo ut instituantur, *secundo ut promulgentur*, tertio ut moribus utentium approbentur; ac si quid horum deficiat non esse legem . . . publicationem esse ultimum actum perficientem legem." Cf. *Summa Theologica*, Ia IIae, q. 90, art. 4.

[13] Passerinus, *ibid.*, nn. 477-478; Fagnanus, *Commentaria*, lib. III, tit. 50, *ne clerici vel monachi saecularibus negotiis se immisceant*, cap. VIII, n. 39.

[14] Mascardus, *De Probationibus*, Vol. II, concl. 640, n. 6; Vol. II, concl. 879, n. 18.

[15] Fagnanus, *Commentaria*, lib. I, tit. *de constitutionibus*, cap. XIII, n. 32, 33.

[16] Gonzalez-Tellez, *Commentaria Perpetua*, ad c. 9, X, *de clerico excommunicato, deposito vel interdicto ministrante*, V, 27, n. 3: "Ignorantia etiam iuris naturalis et gentium omnibus damnabilis est . . . ideo non excusat a delicto, nec a poena." Reiffenstuel, *Jus Canonicum Universum*, ad Reg. 13, R.J., in VI°, n. 14; Mascardus, *De Probationibus*, Vol. II, concl. 640, nn. 4, 5.

nor were any exceptions admitted for certain classes of persons, such as soldiers, women, minors, rustics, etc., when the matter in question concerned ignorance or error of either the natural law or the quasi-natural law, e. g., legislation regarding marriage.[17]

Ignorance of the *positive law* could not be counted as invincible ignorance, for every man was presumed to be able to obtain knowledge of the law either through his own efforts or from those who were acquainted with legal matters.[18]

The commentators considered in detail the knowledge of the law as demanded in virtue of one's place or station in society. Thus they taught that those who occupied offices and positions of responsibility were expected to know the laws which related to the duties of their state. Consequently such persons were not presumed to be ignorant of matters regarding their office, etc.[19] Furthermore, men of nobility, genius or superior education were readily presumed to know the law.[20]

The commentaries indicated that this knowledge was to be expected among those whose way of life was conducive to the acquisition of such knowledge. They placed more emphasis upon knowledge of the law on the part of men than on the part of women; on the part of men who lived a civilian life than on the part of those who led a military life; on the part of the lettered than on the part of the unlettered, etc. Consequently women, soldiers, rustics, minors and the unlearned could allege ignorance

[17] Gonzalez-Tellez, *Commentaria Perpetua*, ad c. 4, X, *de secundis nuptiis*, IV, 21, n. 2; Mascardus, *De Probationibus*, Vol. II, concl. 640, n. 5.

[18] Fagnanus, *Commentaria*, I, tit. *de constitutionibus*, cap. V, n. 427; Gonzalez-Tellez, *Commentaria Perpetua*, lib. V, tit. XXVII, cap. IX, n. 3: ". . . similiter et iuris positivi ignorantia probabilis non est, quia quilibet paterfamilias potest per se, vel peritiores consulendo, scire."

[19] Fagnanus, *Commentaria*, lib. III, tit. *de clerico aegrotante, vel debilitato*, cap. I, n. 47; Passerinus, *Commentaria*, lib. I, cap. II, q. I, art. 25, n. 474.

[20] Passerinus, *ibid.*, n. 475; Fagnanus, *Commentaria*, lib. I, tit. *de constitutionibus*, cap. V, n. 427 seq.

of the law, and if they duly proved their ignorance they were excused from penalties and from the payment of damages.[21]

The authors regarded *ignorance regarding a doubtful law* as ignorance of fact.[22] A law was considered doubtful when its subject-matter could be determined only with difficulty, and when controversies existed regarding its true meaning. Ambiguous words and expressions which suggested a variety of meanings and which gave rise to various and contrary opinions rendered a law doubtful. Regarding such laws one could be presumed to be in excusable ignorance.[23]

However, ignorance regarding a doubtful law offered no basis for an excuse when recourse could be made to those who were skilled in the law.[24] Legal experts, judges and officials were not presumed to be admissibly ignorant of doubtful laws or to be in acknowledgeable error regarding the true legal interpretation of the law. Such error on their part was considered the result of an accountable imprudence, and if in practice these persons put aside the common opinions and followed views which lacked a juridical foundation and thus stood contrary to the law, they were duty-bound to furnish proof of the reasonableness of their acts when founded on such opinions. The presumption of favoring rashness, of straining at singularity, or of nurturing crass or even affected ignorance militated against them.[25]

Ignorance regarding invalidating and disqualifying laws will be considered in the following article.

---

[21] Fagnanus, *Commentaria*, lib. III, tit. *de regularibus*, cap. XXII, n. 10; Gonzalez-Tellez, *Commentaria Perpetua*, ad c. 4, X, *de secundis nuptiis*, IV, 21, 4; Passerinus, *Commentaria*, lib. I, tit. II, cap. II, q. 1, art. 25, n. 475.

[22] Fagnanus, *Commentaria*, lib I, tit. *de constitutionibus*, cap. XIII, n. 33; Mascardus, *De Probationibus*, Vol. I, concl. 120, n. 3; Passerinus, *Commentaria*, lib. I, tit. II, cap. II, q. 1, art. 25, n. 480.

[23] Wernz-Vidal, *Ius Canonicum* (7 vols. in 8, Romae: Apud Aedes Universitatis Gregorianae, 1923-1938), I, n. 189.

[24] Fagnanus, *Commentaria*, lib. I, tit. II, *de constitutionibus*, cap. XIII, n. 49.

[25] Passerinus, *Commentaria*, ibid., n. 483; Fagnanus, *Commentaria*, Lib. I, tit. 2, *de constitutionibus*, cap. XIII, n. 32, and lib. III, tit. 32, *de conversione coniugatorum*, cap. IV, n. 2.

ARTICLE 2. IGNORANCE OF INVALIDATING AND DISQUALIFYING LAWS

The post-Tridentine canonists clearly distinguished between and formally classified the various kinds of laws. Examining various aspects of the concept of law, they distinguished between divine, natural, human, positive, ecclesiastical and civil. Further classifications were also considered. Among these were the categories identified through the *"lex odiosa"* and the *"lex favorabilis."*

Penal law and invalidating law were classified as *"leges odiosae"*; the former was defined as a law for the violation of which a punishment or a fine or both were attached; the latter was delineated as a law which denied efficacy to an act, i.e., rendered it nugatory and null. As an example of an invalidating law the authors frequently and quite spontaneously pointed to the Tridentine decree *Tametsi,* which prescribed that marriages in order to be valid had to be entered according to the form set forth in this decree. These and further subdivisions were treated by the authors.[26]

It seems unnecessary here to discuss the legal doctrines and structure which the canonists developed in regard to the meaning and implications of invalidating and disqualifying laws. But, although the present article is concerned primarily with ignorance in respect to invalidating and disqualifying laws, nevertheless some of the aspects of invalidating and disqualifying laws in themselves must be noted. The canonists, for example, differentiated between invalidating laws which rendered something invalid either directly *(directe)* or indirectly *(indirecte).* Invalidating laws operated *directly* if they contained such phrases as *"irritus est, non valeat, robur et firmitatem non habeat, locum non habeat, etc."*; *indirectly,* if the law prescribed the fulfillment of certain requirements, stipulations or conditions as essential matters without the presence of which the object concerned could not be constituted. Such a re-

[26] Sess. XXIV, *de ref. matrim.,* c. 1; c. Pichler, *Jus Canonicum* (2 vols., Ravennae, 1741), lib. I, tit. II, n. 59; Reiffenstuel, *Jus Canonicum Universum,* Vol. 1, prooemium, §§ 1-4; Schmalzgrueber, *Ius Ecclesiasticum Universum* (5 vols. in 12, Romae, 1843-1845), Vol. I, dissert. prooemium, 3, nn. 86 seq.; Vol. I, dissert. prooem. 4, nn. 112 seq.; Lib. I, tit. 2, nn. 1-7.

quirement, for instance, was any *"conditio sine qua non"* for the completion of a contract.[27]

The same situation was verified in matters in which the Church had declared the faithful incapable of acting, as when the Tridentine legislation declared that clandestine marriages, though up to that time they had been recognized as true marriages, could no longer in the nature of true matrimonial unions be contracted. Clandestine unions had always been detested and forbidden; nevertheless it had remained possible to contract them as valid marriages.[28]

"Inhabilitas" was not a penalty properly so called; rather, it implied the presence of an impediment whereby a person was hindered by law from acquiring rights or barred from the exercise of rights already possessed.[29]

From these considerations it followed that when a law simply forbade some act, and did not at the same time either directly or indirectly imply any invalidating effect, then any act done contrary to such a law was to be considered simply illicit, and not also invalid.[30]

Thus the rule of Pope Innocent III, "multa fieri prohibentur, quae, si facta fuerint, obtinent roboris firmitatem,"[31] became recognized as a sound and permanent rule of law. Accordingly the subject matter and the terminology of the law indicated whether or not a law was invalidating or disqualifying in character. Furthermore, the legislator was recognized as having the right to enact invalidating and disqualifying laws for the sake of the common

---

[27] Pichler, *Jus Canonicum*, lib. I, tit. II, n. 61; Reiffenstuel, *Jus Canonicum Universum*, lib. I, tit. II, n. 243.

[28] Sess. XXIV, *de ref. matrim.*, c. 1.

[29] Santi, *Praelectiones Juris Canonici* (5 vols. in 2, Ratisbonae, Neo-Eboraci et Cincinnattii, 1886), lib. 1, tit. 2, n. 12.

[30] Pichler, *Jus Canonicum*, lib. I, tit. II, nn. 70-71. ". . . legem prohibere tantum, et non irritare simul." Reiffenstuel, *Jus Canonicum Universum*, lib. I, tit. II, n. 244; *op. cit.*, cap. II ad Reg. 64, R.J., in VI°, n. 4. Schmalzgrueber, *Ius Ecclesiasticum Universum*, lib. I, tit. 2, n. 5.

[31] C. 16, X, *de regularibus et transeuntibus ad religionem*, III, 31.

good.[32] He likewise could prohibit acts which, although indifferent in themselves, proved actually harmful to society.[33]

The authors explicitly taught that, although ignorance could excuse from a crime and the penalty attached to it, it could not excuse from the force of invalidating and disqualifying laws. Ignorance could not serve to render invalid acts valid.[34] Thus ignorance of the law was not admitted as an excuse from what the law required for valid matrimonial consent, for the bond of religious profession, or for the valid reception of Sacred Orders.[35] Likewise, those who were bound to observe the specified form for the contracting of marriage were simply incapable *(inhabiles)* of entering a valid marriage in any other manner. If marital consent was exchanged in a manner that was contrary to what was required in the decree *Tametsi,* it was invalid, and ignorance regarding this decree, even invincible ignorance, did not serve to counteract the invalidating force and effect of the decree.[36]

Those laws which derived from the natural law did not need to have any invalidating clauses incorporated in them, since the natural law itself rendered certain acts invalid.[37] Thus marriage

---

[32] Pichler, *Jus Canonicum,* lib. I, tit. II, n. 59; Reiffenstuel, *Jus Canonicum Universum,* lib. I, tit. 2, n. 239; Santi, *Praelectiones Juris Canonici,* lib. I, tit. 2, n. 12.

[33] Santi, *loc cit.*

[34] Fagnanus, *Commentaria,* lib. I, tit. III, de simonia, cap. XXVII, nn. 48-49: ". . . generaliter est ut ignorantia excludat delictum. Tamen non legitimat actum . . . et quamvis excuset a poena, non tamen dat robur actui alias invalido." Cf. Sanchez, *De Matrimonio,* lib. XI, disputatio 32, nn. 7, 15; lib. III, disput. 18, nn. 10-11; Pichler, *Jus Canonicum,* lib. I, tit. 2, n. 67 ". . . ignorantia . . . non tamen impedire potest vim legis, volens actum esse nullum."

[35] Fagnanus, *Commentaria,* lib. III, tit. 31, *de regularibus et transeuntibus ad religionem,* c. XXII, n. 12; S. C. de Religiosis, 30 iul. 1909, ad I—*Acta Apostolicae Sedis, Commentarium Officiale* (Romae, 1909-), I (1909), 699 (hereafter cited *AAS*).

[36] Conc. Trident., sess. XXIV, *de ref. matrim.* c. 1; Sanchez, *De Matrimonio,* lib. III, disp. IV, nn. 9-10; lib. III, disp. XVII, nn. 10-11; Moroni, *Centum Responsa Centum Quaesitis* (Mediolani, 1682), Responsum LVI, n. 107.

[37] Pichler, *Jus Canonicum,* lib. I, tit. II, n. 71; Schmalzgrueber, *Jus Ecclesiasticum Universum,* Vol. I, dissert. prooem. § II, nn. 67, 70.

tam in contracto quam in usu talis matrimonii" was absolutely forbidden to persons who were related to each other in the direct line. The natural law could even absolutely, that is, in relation to any other qualified person, render someone incapable in respect to marriage. Such a disqualification existed for any person whose impotence implied a permanent hindrance to marriage.[38]

The force of invalidating laws extended alike to soldiers and rustics, to women and the minors, even though ignorance on their part could serve to excuse them from the incurring of penalties or the paying of damages.[39] *A fortiori* no others could in consequence of their ignorance ever hope to be excused from invalidating laws. The invalidity of their acts did not depend on the knowledge or lack of knowledge of the law; that effect necessarily inhered in every act through the simple and objective fact of its noncompliance with the law.[40]

For the sake of completeness some mention should be made of the dispute concerning the juridical effect of ignorance on irregularities. Sanchez (1550-1610) in discussing the extent to which ignorance simply of the penalty could be admitted as an excuse, considered it probable that ignorance regarding an "*irregularitas ex delicto*" excused one from incurring it. A number of authors were of the same opinion,[41] but there were also other authors who held that ignorance did not excuse, for they felt that an irregularity was truly of the nature of a personal disqualification.[42]

---

[38] Schmalzgrueber, *Ius Ecclesiasticum Universum*, Vol. 1, dissert. prooem, § II, n. 70.

[39] Fagnanus, *Commentaria*, lib. III, tit. 31, *de regularibus et transeuntibus ad religionem*, cap. XXII, n. 10; Sanchez, *De Matrimonio*, lib. VII, disput. 37, ques. 3, n. 25.

[40] Moroni, *Centum Responsa Centum Quaesitis*, Responsum LVI, n. 107.

[41] Sanchez, *De Matrimonio*, lib. IX, disp. XXXII, nn. 20-21; Schmalzgrueber, *Ius Ecclesiasticum Universum*, lib. V, tit. XXXVII, nn. 107-109; Lehmkuhl, *Theologia Moralis* (5. ed., 2 vols., Friburgi Brisgoviae, 1888), II, 710; S. Alphonsus, *Theologia Moralis* (ed. Gaudé, 4 vols., Romae, 1905-1912), lib. VII, n. 351.

[42] V. gr. Suarez, *De Censuris*, disp. XL, Sect. V, n. 10—*Opera*

ARTICLE 3. IGNORANCE OF THE PENALTY

Besides the distinction between ignorance of law and ignorance of fact, there was the further distinction between either of these and the ignorance in relation to the penalty exclusively. Toso (died 1946) held that this latter category implied an ignorance of law if one did not know in what the penalty consisted, but that it connoted an ignorance of fact if one did not know that the penalty was attached to the law in question.[43]

Before the Code some authors considered the ignorance which related exclusively to the penalty as a form of ignorance of fact.[44] But in whatever manner this type of ignorance was appraised, whether as ignorance of law or as ignorance of fact, its juridical effects were regulated by the norms and principles that applied to these two types of ignorance. In consequence, ignorance as relating solely to the penalty was not presumed. Such ignorance one could indeed allege, but if one did allege it, one furthermore had to establish proof of its existence before it could serve as an excuse.

ARTICLE 4. IGNORANCE OF FACT

Throughout the post-Tridentine period the authors restated the traditional norms and principles in regard to ignorance of fact. The contributions they made were by way of application and clarification of these principles in various and specific circumstances.

Thus it was universally stated that ignorance of fact—which was described as connoting some unforeseen and unapprehended

---

Omnia, XXIII, p. 352; Salmanticenses, *Cursus Theologiae Moralis* (6 vols. in 4, Venetiis, 1714-1728—*De Censuris,* cap. I, punct. XV, n. 195; Thesaurus-Giraldi, *De Poenis Ecclesiasticis* (nova editio, Romae, 1831), Pars I, cap. XV, q. I, n. 2; Pichler, *Candidatus Jurisprudentiae Sacrae* (3. ed., 5 vols., 1723-1728; Vol. I, 4. ed., 1733, Augustoduni), lib. V, tit. XXXVII, n. 25.

[43] *Ad Codicem Iuris Canonici Commentaria Minora,* I (2. ed., Taurini, Romae: Marietti, 1921), p. 39 (hereafter cited *Commentaria Minora*).

[44] Cf., v. gr., Gabriel a S. Vincentio, *De Remediis Ignorantiae* (Romae, 1671), disp. I, dub. I, n. 6.

fact resulting from a human action[45] was not presumed. If alleged ignorance was to prevail against the contrary presumption of the law, it could do so only when the ignorance had become conclusively established as a fact.[46]

In general, everyone was considered to have knowledge of his own acts. Consequently, everyone was presumed not to be in ignorance or in error regarding what he had done.[47] The presumption of non-ignorance was especially strong when the actions had been performed in the recent past, or when the acts in question had been accompanied with some solemnity, as in the case of the reception of Sacred Orders.[48] On the other hand, ignorance could be alleged in regard to certain personal acts performed in the distant past,[49] provided however that these were not of a striking character or of far-reaching importance, or acts of a distinctively intricate or complex nature.[50] Facts of a personal nature which involved obligations to a third party were not presumed to lapse readily from one's memory or to become unknown. The

---

[45] Gonzalez-Tellez, *Commentaria Perpetua*, ad c. 9, X, *de clerico excommunicato, deposito, vel interdicto ministrante*, V, 27, sub notis n. 1: "quando ex actione hominis aliquod factum resultat quod non praevisum nec cognitum fuit."

[46] Gonzalez-Tellez, *ibid.*, n. 3: ". . . ignorantis facti non praesumi . . . et ideo non est probabilis ignorantia, nec excusat, nisi talis probetur." Cf. Passerinus, *Commentaria*, lib. I, cap. II, q. I, art. 25, n. 493.

[47] Mascardus, *De Probationibus*, Vol. I, concl. 325, n. 25: Vol. I, concl. 554, n. 6; Vol. II, concl. 879, n. 40; Vol. II, concl. 641, n. 5; Gonzalez-Tellez, *Commentaria Perpetua*, ad. c. 9, X, *de clerico excommunicato, deposito, vel interdicto ministrante*, V, 27, n. 18: ". . . ignorantia proprii facti immo nec praesumitur"; Barbosa, *Collectanea Doctorum tam Veterum quam Recentiorum in Ius Pontificium Universum* (5 vols. in 3, Lugduni, 1637), lib. I, tit. III, cap. XLI, n. 2 (hereafter cited *Collectanea Doctorum*).

[48] Fagnanus, *Commentaria*, lib. V, tit. *de clerico per saltum promoto*, caput. I, n. 19; Covarrubias, *Opera Omnia*, lib. I, pars II, *Relectionis Initium*, § *de bona et mala fide in praescriptione*, n. 2.

[49] Mascardus, *De Probationibus*, Vol. II, concl. 879, n. 41; *Barbosa*, *loc. cit.*

[50] Mascardus, *ibid.*, nn. 42, 43-45; also Vol. II, concl. 637, n. 22.

same presumption obtained with reference to acts which had been accompanied with an oath.[51]

Possible ignorance regarding one's own performed acts was acknowledged in favor of the Supreme Pontiff and the heads of states in view of the vast scope of their jurisdiction and activity. This rule applied in particular when the matters were of lesser importance.[52] Mascardus (d. 1588) was of the opinion that personal facts which were bound up with a multiplicity of business or confusion could indeed give rise to a presumption of ignorance.[53] He likewise taught that ignorance regarding one's own performed acts could well be acknowledged when one had become beguiled by the act of another, or when one had been led to act through ready persuasion.[54]

Likewise it was presumed that one lacked knowledge concerning certain facts in the lives of others.[55] This presumption admitted of various applications and distinctions, as will be shown in the subsequent paragraphs. With the favor of legal presumption one could not, for instance, allege ignorance in the matters which one was obliged to know.[56] Thus bishops were presumed not to be

---

[51] Mascardus, *De Probationibus*, Vol. II, concl. 879, nn. 43-45, 47.

[52] Gonzalez-Tellez, *Commentaria Perpetua*, ad c. 12, X, *de sententia et re iudicata*, II, 27, n. 10: ". . . regulam illius textus limitari in Summo Pontifice et alio quovis Principe supremo; quia propter implicationem et multitudinem causarum, quae apud ipsos expediuntur, praesumitur probabilis ignorantia et oblivio respectu singulorum . . . sicut aliquando circumstantiis personarum, temporis et negotiorum, etiam *in facto proprio* admittitur iusta ignorantia, seu oblivio praesertim ubi factum non est admodum notabile."

[53] *De Probationibus*, Vol. II, concl. 879, n. 53; Barbosa, *Collectanea Doctorum*, lib. I, tit. III, cap. XLI, n. 2.

[54] *Op cit.*, Vol. II, concl. 879, n. 4: ". . . ignorantia in factor proprio admittatur quando quis inductus fuisset persuasione, vel deceptus facto alterius, ut habemus ex. c. 6, C. 34, q. 2." The canon of the *Decretum Gratiani* referred to by Mascardus is summarized with the words, "Non cogatur legitimam deserere uxorem qui nesciens dormivit cum eius sorore."

[55] Gonzalez-Tellez, *Commentaria Perpetua*, ad c. 9, X, *de. clerico* excommunicato, suspenso vel interdicto ministrante, V, 27, n. 18.

[56] Barbosa, *Cellectanea Doctorum*, lib. I, tit. VI, cap. XX, n. 22; Torre, *De Pactis Futurae Successionis Tractatus Tripartitus* (3 vols. in I, Venetiis, 1694), lib. II, cap. 30, n. 23.

ignorant of the affairs in their own dioceses,[57] such as the vacancy of a benefice.[58] Persons were likewise presumed not to be invincibly ignorant of any matters that were pertinent to their state of life, whether they were religious, pastors, confessors, judges, or others.[59]

However, the law made allowance for the presence of invincible ignorance in regard to matters of great complexity or difficulty. Yet even in this case the person who lacked knowledge had first to show that he had exercised the proper diligence to ascertain the requisite knowledge. Persons who were in positions of responsibility, and whose work demanded that they clarify difficulties and remove doubts, were not favored with any legal presumption of ignorance in consequence simply of the fact that a given situation presented obscurities of one kind or another. However, when a person had endeavored to ascertain the facts diligently, inasmuch as he had used the proper means at his disposal, his lack of knowledge could be presumed to be invincible. Furthermore, the authors readily acknowledged that the knowledge of certain facts could and at times actually did escape even the specialists themselves.[60]

When the fact was of a striking character or belonged to the recent past, then there was a strong presumption of the possession of knowledge.[61] A presumption of ignorance regarding facts in

---

[57] Passerinus, *Commentaria*, lib. I, cap. II, q. I, art. 25, n. 493.

[58] Barbosa, *Pastoralis Solicitudinis sive de Officio et potestate Episcopi* (3 vols. in 1, Lugduni, 1678), Pars III, alleg. CXXVI, n. 48.

[59] Moroni, *Centum Responsa Centum Quaesitis*, Responsum LVI, n. 106; Gonzalez-Tellez, *Commentaria Perpetua*, ad c. 9, X, *de cleric. excomm.*, V, 27, n. 3: ". . . immo nec ignorantia facti alieni excusat, quando ratione officii, vel alio respectu quis tenetur illud investigare . . . haec enim crassa et supina ignorantia iudicatur."

[60] Moroni, *loc. cit.;* Suarez, *De Censuris*, disp. IV, sect. VIII, nn. 12-19—*Opera Omnia*, XXIII, pp. 130-132; Gonzalez-Tellez, *Commentaria Perpetua*, ad c. 9, *de clerico excommunicator, deposito, vel interdicto ministrante*, V, 27, n. 18: ". . .ignorantia facti alieni iusta et probabilis est . . . quia talis ignorantia etiam prudentissimos fallit." Gulielmus Durandus, *Speculum Iuris* (4 vols. in 3, Venetiis, 1577), lib. I, partic. III, *de advocato*, n. 2.

[61] Mascardus, *De Probationibus*, Vol. III, concl. 2197, n. 27; Barbosa, *Praxis Exigendi Pensiones, cui accesserunt Vota Plurima Decisiva et Consultiva Canonica* (Lugduni, 1663)—cf. *Vota Plurima Decisiva*, etc., lib. II, votum LXVIII, n. 46.

the lives of others was not sustained whenever a plea of ignorance regarding such facts would have served one's excuse from an obligation or for one's escape from discomfiture. The same held true whenever the supposition of the possession of knowledge could have served for one's profit or advantage. Thus an heir was presumed not to be ignorant of the facts that rendered him eligible for the obtaining of benefits connected with an inheritance.[62] Facts which applied to notable persons were likewise presumed to be known.[63]

Regarding public facts the presumption of an excusable ignorance was not sustained in the law.[64] Consequently ignorance concerning such facts could be alleged only without the favor of any legal presumption.[65] Ignorance was regarded as *"iniusta,"* or *"improbabilis,"* or also *"dissoluta"* in relation to public facts, for such facts everyone was expected to know; such ignorance was deemed the equivalent of *"lata culpa."*[66]

The inhabitants of the place where the facts had occurred were presumed to be aware of them.[67] What had been announced or disclosed in the home was likewise for the members of the household presumed to be known:[68] similarly all bystanders and witnesses were regarded as having knowledge of the facts which took place in their presence.[69] On the other hand, there was a presumption that one lacked knowledge regarding occult facts in the lives of others.[70] And whenever the law presumed the presence of ignorance in someone's favor, then the burden of proof in dislodging that presumption rested with his adversary.[71]

---

[62] Mascardus, *De Probationibus*, Vol. II, concl. 879, n. 34.

[63] Mascardus, *op cit.* Vol. II, concl. 879, n. 28.

[64] Barbosa, *Collectanea Doctorum*, lib. I, tit. V, cap. 1.

[65] Torre, *De Pactis Futurae Successionis Tractatus Tripartitus*, lib. II, cap. 30, n. 23.

[66] Gonzalez-Tellez, *Commentaria Perpetua*, ad c. 9, X, *de clerico excommunicato, deposito, vel interdicto ministrante*, V, 27, n. 6.

[67] Mascardus, *op. cit.*, Vol. II, concl. 637, n. 14; concl. 879, nn. 15, 28.

[68] Mascardus, *op. cit.*, Vol. II, concl. 879, n. 35.

[69] Mascardus, *ibid.*, n. 38.

[70] Mascardus, *ibid.*, n. 15.

[71] Passerinus, *Commentaria*, lib. I, cap. II, q. I, art. 25, n. 509.

RÉSUMÉ OF THE HISTORICAL DEVELOPMENT

The fundamental principles dealing with ignorance of law and ignorance of fact are to be found in the works of the ancient writers and Fathers of the Church. In their concept of law they emphasized the elements of the inviolability of law and of the necessity of the subject's complete compliance with the demand which was contained in the legal prescription. This doctrine gave rise to the attitude of considering most laws as invalidating or disqualifying in character.

The Penitential Books were influenced in a marked degree by the primitive legal systems. Nevertheless, the principles regarding the subjective elements of law were not completely submerged. Violations of the law when committed in ignorance were punished with mitigated penalties. The defendant had to prove his alleged ignorance by means of some manner of proof. Under these primitive systems the presumed knowledge of the law, of the penalty, of one's own acts, or of the notorious acts of others constituted elements within one and the same general category of legal presumption.

The decretists laid the foundations for a systematized body of principles governing the various aspects of ignorance of law and of ignorance of fact. The doctrine was developed further under the influences of the scholastic theologians and the Roman Law glossators, and then became fully elaborated by the decretalists.

A notable development took place during the Decretalist period in respect to invalidating laws. Several decretals of the *Liber Sextus* set a new course for the future, and gave rise to specific teachings which became an important contribution to the canon law doctrine on invalidating and disqualifying laws.

The sixteenth century initiated the achievement of the subsequent centuries, that is, the complete and systematic exposition of the principles and norms relative to ignorance of law and ignorance of fact. There were, of course, disputed opinions, and also gradual shifts in one direction or another on the part of

[73] Canon 988. Cf. Vermeersch-Creusen, *Epitome Iuris Canonici* (3 vols., Vol. I, 6. ed., 1937, Vols. II-III, 5. ed., 1934-1936, Romae, Mechliniae: H. Dessain), II, 171.

canonical authors. Differences of opinion existed, for example, on the influence of ignorance with reference to the contracting of irregularities. It remained for the Code of Canon Law to determine the nature of irregularities and to settle the doubt concerning ignorance by expressly declaring that ignorance does not excuse.[72] Thus in the codification of the present law of the Church these differences were solved, and the generally accepted canonical doctrines of the preceding centuries were made succinctly and authoritatively explicit.

PART TWO

Canonical Commentary

CHAPTER V

THE NATURE AND THE DIVISIONS OF IGNORANCE

Before one proceeds to analyze under separate headings each of the two paragraphs of canon 16, it is necessary to study in some detail the nature and the divisions of ignorance. Some of the following considerations may seem superfluous; however, inasmuch as the various kinds and manifestations of ignorance are referred to, at least by name, in other parts of this work, it is necessary that their significance be explained, and this chapter has been chosen as the most logical place to consider them.

ARTICLE 1. THE NATURE OF IGNORANCE

The word *ignorance* is derived from the Latin *ignorare,* meaning not to know (a person or thing), to have no knowledge of, to mistake.[1] The word *ignorare* in turn is derived from the Greek αγνοεω, meaning not to perceive or know, to be ignorant of, to forget, to escape notice.[2] When considered in the broad sense, ignorance connotes any absence or negation of knowledge. In this sense irrational and nonintellectual beings can be said to be ignorant; however, ignorance in its more exact meaning signifies the absence of pertinent knowledge; it is the lack *(carentia* or *privatio)* of knowledge which one ought to have. Thus, ignorance in the proper sense of the term can be predicated only of intellectual beings, since they alone have both the ability and inherent aptitude for attaining knowledge.

In the light of a psychological analysis of the concept of ignorance the knowledge which a person should have is that

[1] *Harper's Latin Dictionary* (revised by C. T. Lewis and C. Short, New York: American Book Co., 1879, s. v. *ignorare.*

[2] H. G. Liddell—R. Scott, *Greek-Latin Lexicon* (8. ed., New York: American Book Co., 1897), s. v. αγνοεω.

knowledge which is consequent upon his human nature. A human being should possess knowledge in so far as knowledge is a natural perfection of his being. This obligation to know pertains primarily and radically to a natural perfection as distinct from a moral perfection or a moral obligation. Thus St. Thomas defined ignorance as a privation of knowledge of those things which one is naturally equipped and constituted to know.[3] According to this definition ignorance is restricted exclusively to those who are capable of acquiring knowledge. Not only must the subject have the natural faculty to know, but he must be habitually and actually capable of exercising that faculty. Thus insane persons cannot properly be designated as ignorant; infants likewise because of their mental immaturity cannot be considered to be ignorant.

Another definition of ignorance employed by a great number of authors is that in which ignorance is described as a lack of the knowledge which one can and should have.[4] The knowledge which one can and is obliged to possess according to the proponents of this definition is that knowledge which should be present by reason of one's human nature.[5]

It frequently happens that authors apply the term ignorance to subjective states of the mind which if rightly appraised should not be so regarded.[6] Thus suspicion, opinion and doubt are classi-

---

[3] St. Thomas, *Summa Theologica,* Ia IIae, q. 76, art. 2: "... ignorantia . . . importat scientiae privationem, dum scilicet alicui deest scientia eorum, quae aptus natus est scire." Cf. Passerinus, *Commentaria,* lib. I, tit. II, cap. II, q. I, art. 1; Vermeersch, *Theologiae Moralis Principia* (3. ed., Romae: Universitas Gregoriana, 1933-1937), I, 72 (hereafter cited *Theologia Moralis*); Wernz-Vidal, *Ius Canonicum,* VII, 91; Michiels, *Normae Generales Juris Canonici* (2 vols., Lublin: Universitas Catholica, 1929), I, 348 (hereafter cited *Normae Generales*).

[4] St. Thomas, *De Malo,* q. 8, art. 1, ad. 7. Cf. Ojetti, *Commentarium in Codicem Iuris Canonici* (4 vols., Romae: Universitas Gregoriana, 1927-1931), I, 127 (hereafter cited *Commentarium*); Blat, *Commentarium Textus Codicis Iuris Canonici* (6 vols., Romae, 1921-1927); Liber V, *De Delictis et Poenis* (Romae: Collegio "Angelico," 1924, p. 27 (hereafter cited *De Delictis et Poenis*); Michiels, *Normae Generales,* I, 348.

[5] Cf. Passerinus, *Commentaria,* lib. I, tit. II, cap. II, q. I, art. 1.

[6] Cf. Passerinus, *Commentraia,* lib. I, tit. II, cap. II, q. I, art. 1, n. 60.

fied under the general term "ignorance," but these states of mind are vastly different. Ignorance admits of various degrees depending upon the amount of knowledge an individual may possess in regard to some matter. A person may possess knowledge of certain aspects of some truth and be ignorant of others. Men differ in their experience and powers of perception.

A person who *suspects* something to be true gives his assent, but only with the highest degree of hesitation for the reason that the opposite may be true. An *opinion* is the assent which the mind gives to one of two or more contradictory propositions, yet not without fear of the truth of the opposite.[7] One in such a state of mind makes a reasonable choice, but only timidly and without certitude.[8] Since law is concerned with actions, and actions presuppose a judgment, in law the words "doubt" and "opinion" are oftentimes used synonymously.[9]

ARTICLE 2. IGNORANCE AND ERROR AND INADVERTENCE

Ignorance and error differ one from the other philosophically. Psychologically considered, only the complete lack of knowledge can be defined as ignorance. Ignorance is complete when one has never become aware of the truth at all. On the other hand, ignorance may be only partial in so far as knowledge and ignorance may coexist in an individual in regard to the same matter viewed under different aspects. A truth may be partially known and partially unknown. However, error is a false judgment; it is an assent of the mind to a false proposition, a positive denial of the objective truth.[10]

Although vastly different, the two are closely correlated, so that error is always the result of ignorance, with the exception of those cases when the mind is influenced by passion or prejudice. Igno-

---

[7] J. S. Hickey, *Summula Philosophiae Scholasticae* (3 vols., Dublin, 1919), I, n. 161.

[8] Hickey, *op. cit.*, I, n. 161.

[9] Lucius Ferraris, *Prompta Bibliotheca Canonica, Iuridica, Moralis, Theologica, nec non Ascetica, Polemica, Rubricistica, Historica* (9 vols., Romae, 1885-1899), s. v. *conscientia*, n. 22 seq.

[10] Cf. St. Augustinus, *Enchiridion ad Laurentium*, c. 17—*MPL*, XL, 239—c. 11, D. XXXVIII: ". . . non tamen est consequens ut continuo

rance is an outstanding source of error,[11] which is ignorance in action.[12]

In so far as error is a false judgment, it proceeds from ignorance as its cause. This cause and effect relationship between ignorance and error prompts canonists to attribute the same juridical effect to the two.[13] The Code canonized this principle in the fifth book, where it is stated that what is said of ignorance applies equally to inadvertence and error.[14] In general, ignorance may be considered a technical term designating both ignorance and error. Thus canonical ignorance has a wider extension than the strict philosophical definition of ignorance admits. The canonical concept has a foundation in fact, since in the ultimate analysis ignorance is the source and foundation of error. However, ignorance and error are not universally equivalent throughout the entire Canon Law system. For example, the ignorance considered in canon 2247, § 3, in reference to a confessor absolving from a reserved censure is not identical with or universally applicable to error.[15]

Error is of two types, substantial and accidental. Substantial error pertains to the substance of a thing, an act, a law, etc., e.g.,

---

erret quisquis aliquid nescit, sed quisquis se existimat scire quod nescit. Pro vero quippe approbat falsum, quod est erroris proprium." Cf. also Alexander Halensis, *Summa Theologica,* lib. II, P. II, inq. III, tract. I, sect. I, q. II, tit. I, c. 3.

[11] "Ignorantia mater est erroris . . ."—Maroto, *Institutiones Iuris Canonici* (2 vols., 1919; Vol. I, 3. ed., 1921, Romae: Apud Commentarium pro Religiosis), I, 465.

[12] Toso, "De Errore Communi," *Jus Pontificium* (Romae, 1921-1940), III (1923), 150.

[13] Vermeersch-Creusen, *Epitome Iuris Canonici,* I, n. 197: "In iure tamen aequiparantur."; Wernz-Vidal, *Ius Canonicum,* II, n. 39: "In iure tamen idem efficiunt." Cf. Schmalzgrueber, *Jus Ecclesiasticum Universum,* VIII, n. 433; Maroto, *Institutiones Iuris Canonici,* I, n. 87; Michiels, *Normae Generales,* I, 348: ". . . . status erroris, cum ignorantia regulariter conjunctus vel saltem ex ipsa natus; quia error nihil aliud est quam ignorantia positiva, seu falsum de aliqua re judicium."

[14] Canon 2202, § 3.

[15] Cf. Galtier, "De ignorantia et errore in censurarum specialissimo modo reservatarum absolutione," *Periodica,* XVII (1928), 55*-68*.

if someone deliberately wounds a cleric whom he thinks to be a lay person, or if someone submits to subdeaconship thinking that he may later enter a marriage contract. Accidental error pertains to secondary matters, *accessoria* as they are called.[16]

Experience shows that man does not remain in conscious possession of all the truths he had once acquired. Man's awareness of some facts is shortlived. Furthermore, the mind is incapable of adverting fully to but one matter at a time. Human forgetfulness and inadvertence have their roots in man's natural limitations.

In inadvertence the mind fails to give attention either to the physical act itself, or to its moral character, or both. The more serious the matter is, the more does it call for earnest concentration. Forgetfulness and inadvertence can give rise to grave and disastrous consequences. Psychologically considered, inadvertence differs from ignorance in so far as the former presupposes that a person has sufficient knowledge to evaluate his act correctly, but fails to apply this knowledge. Inadvertence implies that an individual actually possesses the knowledge but fails to apply it, whereas ignorance in the strictest sense points to the fact that the individual never became aware of some truth. Authors in considering the various causes from which inadvertence rises distinguish separate species under the general heading of inadvertence. Some of the causes are rotted in man's physical and psychic constitution; others are extraneous but nevertheless under his indirect or remote control.

Certain human experiences after a lapse of time can neither be recognized nor recalled, while others can only be recognized. Proficiency to recognize and recall past experiences admits of degrees. Inadvertence which results from lapses of memory is referred to as *oblivio* or *oblivio actualis*.[17]

The mind can advert fully to but one matter at a time. It occa-

---

[16] Cf. Toso, *Commentaria Minora*, I, 39; Ojetti, *Commentarium*, I, 131; Michiels, *Normae Generales*, I, 349.

[17] Cf. A. Van Hove, *De Legibus Ecclesiasticis* (Mechiliniae: H. Dessain, 1930), p. 239; M. Lega, *De Delictis et Poenis* (2. ed., Romae), p. 66; Suarez, *De Censuris*, disp. IV, sect. VIII, n. 5—*Opera Omnia*, XXIII, p. 128.

sionally happens that in consequence of his preoccupation with other affairs an individual is prevented from giving adequate attention to a particular action or even to a series of actions. Thus a priest in a parish may become so absorbed in his parochial duties that he may easily forget that he has made a particular appointment unless he keeps a record of the same. This type of inadvertence is often referred to as inattention, preoccupation, absent-mindedness or the Latin *inconsideratio.*[18]

Inadvertence may also arise from a habitual indifference toward law and the attendant responsibility for one's actions. This disregard for the law and for the consequences of one's actions is designated as *incuria.*[19]

Some authors[20] refer to inadvertence as non-habitual ignorance or actual ignorance; however, ignorance is not inadvertence in the strict sense, since the latter presupposes knowledge. Moreover, both ignorance and inadvertence are actual, for both exist at the moment the act is placed.

ARTICLE 3. DOUBT

By way of clarification a short article on the nature and kinds of doubt may prove helpful in this chapter. Although doubt is oftentimes associated and identified with ignorance,[21] it is wrong to identify them always. The Code does not always use them

[18] Cf. Pellé, *Le Droit Pénal de l'Eglise* (Paris: Lethielleux, 1939), p. 13.

[19] Cf. c. 7, X, *de poenitentiis et remissionibus*, V, 38: *ex incuria ipsorum* is contrasted with *ipsis procurantibus vel studiose negligentibus.*

[20] V. gr., Cicognani, *Canon Law* (authorized English version, by J. O'Hara and F. Brennan, 2. revised ed., Phila.: Dolphin Press, 1935), p. 590; Suarez, *De Censuris*, disp. IV, sect. VIII, n. 5—*Opera Omnia*, XXIII, p. 128.

[21] St. Bonaventura, *Commentaria in IV Libros Sententiarum* (ed. minor, ad Claras Aquas: Typographia Collegii S. Bonaventurae, 1934-1938), lib. II, dist. XXII, art. 2: ". . . qui dubitat de aliquo de quo debet esse certus, potius dicitur illud ignorare quam scire." Coronata (*Institutiones Iuris Canonici*, I [2. ed., Taurini: Marietti, 1939] p. 42) describes ignorance in general as: "status mentis inter duo contraria haerentis ancipitis."

in the same manner. Thus canon 15 states that when a doubt of law is present, laws, even though they are invalidating or disqualifying, do not bind. On the other hand, canon 16 provides that ignorance of invalidating or disqualifying laws does not excuse.

Doubt is defined as a state of mind that withholds assent to a proposed question, or as a suspension of judgment between two or more contradictory propositions because of the fear of erring.[22] In the *positive doubt* there still remains a good reason for a prudent man to refrain from giving firm assent. In the *negative doubt* the mind fails to assent to one of the propositions, although the reason for the hesitation is negligible, frivolous or even non-existent.

The doubt of law which exempts one from the observance of a law, even one which is invalidating and disqualifying (canon 15), must be both objective and positive, that is, it must be supported by a valid reason and have a solid foundation in fact.[23] The doubt may concern the existence, the meaning, or the cessation of the law. Thus a doubt of law is present when it is controverted whether an excommunication is of a *latae* or a *ferendae sententiae* character; or the doubt may concern the very existence of a penalty in respect to a certain law.[24] Canon 15 is concerned with objective doubt in the sense that the law itself is not clear, or that the fact from an objective viewpoint is not envisioned as being clearly within the scope of the law.[25] Doubt is subjective when in reality there is no doubtful law or doubtful fact; this doubt exists in the mind alone. Negative and subjective doubt is regarded as ignorance, and consequently should not be identified with the doubt of law and of fact mentioned in canon 15, but should be treated under canon 16.

---

[22] Philippus Maroto, *Institutiones Iuris Canonici*, I, n. 730; Vermeersch-Creusen, *Epitome Iuris Canonici*, I, n. 284.

[23] Cf. Cappello, *Summa Iuris Canonici* (3 vols., Vol. I, 4. ed., 1945; Vol. III, 2. ed., 1940, Romae: Apud Aedes Universitatis Gregorianae), I, n. 93; Cicognani, *Canon Law*, p. 587.

[24] Veermersch-Creusen, *Epitome Iuris Canonici*, I, n. 86.

[25] Cf. Cicognani, *Canon Law*, p. 585.

ARTICLE 4. DIVISIONS OF IGNORANCE

The preceding articles treated the nature of ignorance as such, also error, suspicion, opinion, inadvertence and doubt, all of which are not ignorance in the strict sense, but manifestations or modes of ignorance. Error, suspicion, opinion and doubt arise from ignorance, while inadvertence is a temporary defect or lack in the application of one's knowledge. However, what is said of ignorance is generally applicable also to these mental states.

The present article will treat the various divisions of ignorance which are applicable to the law of canon 16. Numerous divisions of ignorance have been constructed by canonists and moralists in the past; some of these are only of historical importance or interest. This article treats of the more outstanding divisions; the others need not be considered here.

It is intended that the following presentation and analysis will provide a list of the types of ignorance which do not excuse from invalidating and disqualifying laws. These considerations will also furnish some material for the interpretation of the presumptions of law as expressed in canon 16, § 2.

From the time of Suarez (d. 1617), canonists have considered in a special manner four sets of divisions of ignorance; namely, antecedent-concomitant-consequent, involuntary-voluntary, invincible-vincible, and inculpable-culpable. For practical purposes they have favored the last three sets, while the Code has expressly employed only the culpable-inculpable division. However, some post-Code authors refer exclusively to the vincible-invincible division, or employ it as practically synonymous with the division in the Code.[26] The threefold division of antecedent-concomitant-consequent ignorance pertains to the influence of ignorance upon the will. St. Thomas Aquinas furnished the classical analysis of this division in his *Summa Theologica*.[27] *Antecedent ignorance* is

---

[26] Cf. Albertus Cipollini, *De Censuris Latae Sententiae iuxta Codicem Iuris Canonici* (Taurini: Marietti, 1925), p. 21; I. Chelodi, *Ius Poenale et Ordo Procedendi in Iudiciis Criminalibus* (4. ed., a V. Dalpioz, Tridenti: Ardesi, 1935), p. 31; J. Sole, *De Delictis et Poenis* (Romae: Pustet, 1920), pp. 23, 80.

[27] *Summa*, Ia IIae, q. 6, art. 8. Cf. Vermeersch, *Theologia Moralis*, I, 75-78.

involuntary ignorance which causes a man to will something which he would not otherwise will, i.e., if he really knew the fact or situation he would not have acted. On the other hand, a person who places an act while in *concomitant ignorance* would have so acted even if he had known. *Consequent ignorance* is voluntary ignorance which may come about in two ways: first when the ignorance is directly willed (affected ignorance), or secondly, this type of ignorance may arise from some passion or habit or when one neglects to acquire the knowledge which he ought to have.[28]

Of the four divisions of ignorance this division alone lays specific stress on what would have happened had the individual not been ignorant. The legislator does not provide for such hypothetical contingencies, and canonists themselves have generally ignored this distinction and have given their attention to the three divisions which follow.

Of the three sets of divisions of ignorance, the voluntary-involuntary division is least frequently referred to by the authors. Voluntary ignorance is that ignorance which is deliberately chosen by the will, whereas involuntary ignorance cannot be ascribed to the will. In itself this distinction prescinds from any obligation on the part of an individual to know.

The vincible-invincible division is founded on one's ability or effort to use the proper means of acquiring the knowledge and thereby to remove the ignorance.[29] One labors in invincible ignorance when it is either physically or morally impossible for one to overcome it. This distinction considered in itself is not directed toward one's duty or obligation to overcome the ignorance; however, authors understand it to refer only to knowledge which one is bound to possess.[30] Of all the divisions of ignorance most frequently used, the distinction between vincible and invincible ignorance is the most common. As already mentioned above, some authors use it exclusively, while others consider it synonymous with the culpable-inculpable division.[31]

---

[28] Cf. Vermeersch, *loc. cit.*; Michiels, *Normae Generales*, I, 352.

[29] Cf. Vermeersch, *Theologia Moralis*, I, 72-73; Michiels, *Normae Generales*, I, 349.

[30] Cf. Passerinus, *Commentaria*, lib. I, tit. II, cap. II, art. 5; Swoboda, *Ignorance in Relation to the Imputability of Delicts*, p. 130, note 44.

[31] Cf. *supra*, p. 64.

The Code has canonized the culpable-inculpable division of ignorance. The legislator in choosing the words *culpabilis* and *inculpabilis* intended to estimate ignorance according to strictly subjective or moral requirements.

Culpable ignorance may be defined as a morally imputable lack of a knowledge which is both possible and necessary, and because of which lack of knowledge one foresees that he is placing himself in a proximate danger of violating the law. The obligation to overcome the ignorance must be both physically and morally possible through the exercise of a degree of diligence which would be employed by a prudent man under the same facts and circumstances. Furthermore, the person in culpable ignorance must have a moral obligation to know either the law or the facts about which he is ignorant. Consequently, he must be compelled by some necessity to have the knowledge which he lacks.[82]

When a person is about to perform an act, there arises an obligation to know the laws or facts governing or influencing the admissibility of the act he intends to perform. He cannot be guilty of culpable ignorance unless he fails in his obligation to know the laws relative to his act, or in his obligation to know the facts which are pertinent to his action. It is important to note that the law can very frequently be discovered before the necessity for acting arises, while facts must often be investigated at the very time the act is about to be placed. Hence ignorance of fact is less culpable and more readily admissible in the external forum.[83]

A person in culpable ignorance must realize that he is ignorant. He must see, at least in a confused manner, that he may violate the law in consequence of his lack of pertinent knowledge. If a man does not suspect or doubt that he is acting contrary to some legal command or prohibition, his ignorance is purely antecedent to the will and consequently cannot be considered culpable.[84] The degrees of culpable ignorance depend upon a number of factors, such as the nature of the law governing the action to be

[82] Swoboda, *op. cit.*, pp. 132-135.

[83] Cf. Franz Heiner, *Katholisches Kirchenrecht* (5. ed., 2 vols., Paderborn, 1909, II, 85; Hollweck, *Die kirchlichen Strasgesetze* (Mainz, 1899), note 1 to § 16, p. 78.

[84] Vermeersch, *Theologia Moralis*, I, 78.

placed, the difficulties which one must diligently try to overcome in order to dispel the ignorance, and the strength of the suspicion or doubt by which the individual becomes aware of his state of ignorance.[35]

Notwithstanding the manifold degrees of culpable ignorance that may exist in concrete cases, the law distinguishes four distinct degrees of culpable ignorance.[36] Two of these degrees the Code expressly mentions, namely, affected and crass or supine ignorance.[37] Canon 2229, § 3, n. 1, implies a third type of culpable ignorance, which is not crass or supine. It is that which is gravely culpable in character, since it suffices for the incurring of a vindictive penalty, and penalties cannot be inflicted or incurred unless there is grave imputability present.[38] The fourth type of culpability is that which is venially or slightly culpable, and may be deduced from a comparison of canons 2202, § 1, and canon 2229, § 3, n. 1, with canon 2218, § 2. Commentaries and manuals describe these categories of culpable ignorance in the traditional manner. Affected ignorance is that which is deliberately and purposely willed; crass or supine ignorance implies that an individual has the highest degree of negligence, disregard or indifference toward the removal of the ignorance; grave ignorance implies not the absence of all effort to dispel it, but rather the lack of such diligence as a prudent person under the same circumstances would certainly employ in the effort to acquire the necessary knowledge; all ignorance of a lesser degree than that of any and all of the foregoing is venially culpable ignorance.

1. Affected Ignorance

Affected ignorance is that ignorance which is deliberately and purposely sought. It is the deliberate will not to investigate the law or some fact. The word *affected* derives from the Latin *affectare*

[35] Vermeersch, *Theologia Moralis,* I, 77; H. Noldin-A. Schmitt, *Summa Theologiae Moralis* (3 vols.; Vol. I, 26. ed., 1939; Vols. II-III, 25. ed., 1938, Oeniponte: Rauch), I, 58.

[36] Cf. canons 2202; 2223, § 3, n. 3; 2229.

[37] Canon 2229, § 1; 2229, § 3, n. 1.

[38] Cf. canon 2218, § 2; Michiels, *Normae Generales,* I, 350.

or *adfectare,* meaning "to strive after a thing, to exert one's self to obtain, to pursue, to desire."[39]

Affected ignorance is similar to pretense or assumed artifice. It is, moreover, real ignorance and not simply pretended ignorance. It is not by any means equivalent to deceit, in which case an individual is not ignorant at all. With reference to necessary knowledge affected ignorance denoted the lack of such knowledge which is directly willed and procured by positive effort either out of contempt of the law or out of fear lest knowledge would influence one to act otherwise.[40] The person is actually intent upon being ignorant; the ignorance does not merely accompany negligence; the individual exerts himself in order not to have the required knowledge. Ignorance which is the consequence of practically total neglect or of a high degree of neglect is described either as crass or grave ignorance respectively.[41]

Psychologically considered, affected ignorance is simply the direct pursuit of ignorance by positive means. In itself the knowledge which one tries to avoid becoming aware of need not be of obligation; nor need the person strive to be ignorant from wrongful motives. Affected ignorance sometimes merits praise and may, furthermore, be of obligation. The Legion of Decency in respect to motion pictures fosters affected ignorance in matters in which knowledge might well prove to be harmful and dangerous.[42] However, the term *affected ignorance* usually connotes a type of culpable ignorance.[43]

Culpable affected ignorance concerns the lack of a knowledge

---

[39] *Harper's Latin Dictionary,* s. v. *affectare.*

[40] Cf. St. Thomas, *Summa Theologica,* Ia IIae, q. 76, art. 4; Noldin-Schmitt, *Summa Theologiae Moralis,* I, 59; Michiels, *Normae Generales* I, 351; Vermeersch, *Theologia Moralis,* I, 73; Van Hove, *De Legibus Ecclesiasticis,* p. 244; Vermeersch-Creusen, *Epitome Iuris Canonici,* I, n. 88; Blat, *Commentarium Textus Codicis Iuris Canonici* (5 vols. in 6, Liber I, *Normae Generales,* Romae: Collegio "Angelico," 1921), I, 94 (hereafter cited *Normae Generales*).

[41] Cf. Reiffenstuel, *Tractatus de Regulis Juris,* cap. II, R. J. 13 in VI°, n. 7; Sole, *De Delictis et Poenis,* p. 80.

[42] Vermeersch-Creusen, *Epitome Iuris Canonici,* I, n. 88.

[43] Vermeersch, *Theologia Moralis,* I, 73: ". . . nomen affectatae ignorantiae reservari consuevit ignorantiae quae culpanda est."

which is of obligation, and the seeking of this lack rises from a wrong intention. It is unreasonable to expect everyone to have constant knowledge of all the laws. Oftentimes the obligation to know some laws arises only when an individual is about to place a particular act. A person may deliberately choose to remain in ignorance regarding the legislation which does not apply to him. However, whenever an obligation to investigate the law arises and an individual deliberately chooses to remain ignorant, his ignorance must be considered as issuing from a wrong intention. An individual may pursue affected ignorance for numerous reasons; for example, he may wish to excuse his subsequent violation of the law, or he may wish to consider himself free from legal prescriptions, or he may desire even to show contempt for lawful authority through a deliberate disregard for the prescriptions of lawful superiors.

2. *Ignorance as a Consequence of Negligence*

Crass or supine, grave and venial ignorance follow as a result of negligence. These forms of ignorance are distinguished one from the other according to the degree of negligence from which they arise.

Crass ignorance, etymologically considered, points to the mental state of a rude or uncultured person.[44] Likewise the word "supine" in regard to ignorance refers to the state of mind of a careless, thoughtless, heedless or negligent individual.[45] Both of these terms have been used synonymously by canonists,[46] and all canonists are agreed that crass or supine ignorance results from negligence. However, some commentators simply state that it arises from the highest degree of negligence.[47]

---

[44] Literally this word this "thick, dense, heavy"—*Harper's Latin Dictionary*, s. v. *crassus*.

[45] Literally the word "supine" means "bent backwards, lying on the back in bed"—*op. cit.*, s. v. *supinus*.

[46] Cf. Reiffenstuel, *Tractatus de Regulis Juris*, R. J. 13 in VI°, in n. 7.

[47] Among the pre-Code authors there are such names as: Lega, *De Delictis et Poenis*, p. 64; Lehmkuhl, *Theologia Moralis*, II, 621. Among some of the post-Code authors are Salucci, *Il Diritto Penale*

The other element which enters into the concept of crass ignorance pertains to the obligation one has of investigating the law or the fact. Vermeersch (1858-1936)[48] expresses the view that the object of the investigation must be a matter that can easily be learned. Only ignorance of those things which can easily be discovered is to be considered crass or supine. This opinion had long been the traditional doctrine.[49]

Further consideration of crass ignorance in its relation to culpably grave ignorance will be given in the following paragraphs.

Canon 2229, § 3, n. 1, refers to a degree of culpable ignorance which is neither crass nor supine, but which is adequate for the incurring of a vindictive penalty. **Canon 2218, § 3, indicates** that a penalty cannot be contracted for anything less than grave imputability. Consequently the ignorance mentioned in canon 2229, § 3, n. 1, is of necessity a grave ignorance and at the same time distinct from the ignorance that is crass or supine. Thus the Code admits a distinction between grave and crass ignorance, which distinction had formerly been a matter of dispute.[50]

Before the Code many authors, foremost among them Suarez,[51] rejected the distinction completely. St. Alphonsus (1696-1787)[52] regarded the opinion as Suarez as probable.[53] The difficulty of

---

secondo il Codice di Diritto Canonico (2 vols., Subiaco: Tipografia dei Monasteri, 1926-1930), I, 140 (hereafter cited *Il Diritto Penale*); Sole, *De Delictis et Poenis*, p. 80; and others.

[48] *Theologia Moralis*, I, 73; c. Van Hove, *De Legibus Ecclesiasticis*, p. 239.

[49] Cf. Sanchez, *De Matrimonio*, lib. IX, disp. XXXII, n. 33; Panormitanus, *Commentaria*, c. 9, X, *de clerico excommunicato, deposito, vel interdicto ministrante*, V, 27, n. 3.

[50] Some post-Code authors seem to deny the distinction; v. g., Cipollini, *De Censuris Latae Sententiae*, p. 21; Pighi, *Censurae Sententiae Latae et Irregularitates* (7. ed., Veronae: Sorores Cinquetti Filiae Felicis, 1922), p. 8; Prümmer, *Manuale Theologiae Moralis* (8. ed., cura Engelberti Münch, 3 vols., e Friburgi Brisgoviae: Herder, 1935-1936), III, 353; Swoboda, *Ignorance in Relation to the Imputability of Delicts*, p. 145.

[51] *De Censuris*, disp. IV, sect. X, n. 12—*Opera Omnia*, XXIII, p. 142; cf. Michiels, *Normae Generales*, I, 350.

[52] *Theologia Moralis*, lib. VII, n. 45.

[53] Other authors are: Hollweck, *Die kirchlichen Strafgesetze*, note 5

distinguishing crass from grave ignorance derived from the lack of any practical criterion that could have been used as a determining factor for either type of ignorance.[54] However, the Code distinguished between grave and crass ignorance, but without indicating the specific difference between these two types of ignorance. It remained with the commentators to define and elaborate upon this distinction. Thus crass ignorance was distinguished from grave ignorance on the basis that in the former type a person uses no diligence whatever to learn the truth.[55] This opinion is not without implicit foundation among the authors before the Code. Crass ignorance is described as resulting from excessively grave negligence or from a negligence so great that the person who is ignorant should be considered most negligent.[56]

It seems, therefore, that the legislator has sanctioned the opinion of those authors who maintained a real distinction between the two types of ignorance, and thus grave ignorance is distinguished from crass ignorance in so far as the former is characterized by a lack of diligence which is not total, but which lacks equalling the diligence which a prudent man would exercise under the same conditions. Furthermore, the negligence must imply the guilt of grave sin; grave ignorance does not pertain to matters of light moral content. Finally, the object of the ignorance must be a matter the knowledge of which can be readily investigated. Therefore a person is guilty of crass ignorance when he fails to use any effort whatever to obtain the necessary knowledge, when at

---

to § 15, p. 77; Wernz, *Ius Decretalium* (2. ed., 6 vols., Romae et Prati, 1906-1913), VI, p. 31, note 79.

[54] Michiels, *Normae Generales*, I, 350.

[55] Cf. H. A. Ayrinhac—P. J. Lydon, *Penal Legislation in the New Code of Canon Law* (revised ed., New York: Benziger, 1936), p. 9; Cerato, *Censurae Vigentes Ipso Facto a Codice Iuris Canonica Excerptae* (2. ed., Patavii: Typis Seminarii, 1921), p. 50 (hereafter cited *Censurae Vigentes*); Roberti, *De Delictis et Poenis* (vol. I, pars 1, 1930; pars 2, 1938, Romae: Libraria Pontificii Instituti Utriusque Iuris), I, pars 2, p. 106; Van Hove, *De Legibus Ecclesiasticis*, p. 239; and others.

[56] Cf. Lega, *De Delictis et Poenis*, p. 64; Lehmkuhl, *Theologia Moralis*, II, 621.

the same time the knowledge can be obtained through no grave or serious effort on his part.[57]

Venially culpable ignorance is estimated according to the principles of moral theology. In so far as this type of ignorance issues from an omission of due care, it is to be considered culpable; nevertheless, in so far as the penal law is concerned, a venially culpable ignorance is an inculpable ignorance, since circumstances which excuse from grave guilt excuse also from penalties.[58] Consequently those degrees of ignorance which are not sufficient to render a person liable to a penalty according to canon 2218, § 2, constitute no more than a venially culpable ignorance.[59]

3. *Ignorance of the Law, of the Penalty, and of Fact in General*

The Code in canon 16, § 2, makes three legal distinctions in respect to the unknown object, namely, ignorance of law, of the penalty, and of fact. The canon further distinguishes ignorance of fact into ignorance of *facta propria,* of *facta aliena notoria* and of *facta aliena non notoria.* The Code does not define any of these terms, and therefore it is necessary to derive the definitions from the traditional concepts regarding these types of ignorance.

Ignorance of law simply denotes that ignorance which is present when the existence, the sense or the scope of the law are not known. In *ignorance of fact* one does know that a certain concrete object (person or thing) or the circumstance of an object (person or thing) which demand an application of the law are present.[60]

Ignorance of law may be present in those instances in which the law itself is not clear. On the other hand, the law may be clear objectively, but an individual may be ignorant of its meaning

[57] Cf. Michiels, *Normae Generales,* I, 350-351.

[58] Cf. canon 2218, § 2; Coronata, *Institutiones Iuris Canonici* (5 vols.; Vols. I-II, 2. ed., 1939; Vols. III-V, 1933-1936, Taurini: Marietti), I, 43.

[59] Vermeersch-Creusen, *Epitome Iuris Canonici,* I, n. 89.

[60] These concepts are found throughout the authors. The following names are mentioned: St. Thomas, *De Malo,* q. III, a. 8; *Michiels, Normae Generales,* I, 348; Noldin-Schmitt, *Summa Theologiae Moralis,* I, n. 49; Vermeersch, *Theologia Moralis,* I, p. 74.

or extension, or even of its existence. In ignorance of fact the individual fails to evaluate properly the facts as an object of specific legislation. This may be due to the doubtful character of the facts themselves.

It is apparent that both ignorance of law and ignorance of fact may be found together in the same case. For example, a thief may not know that he is forbidden by law to enter the enclosure in a monastery, and furthermore he may not know that he is within the enclosure.

The Code does not use the traditional expressions *ignorantia iuris* and *ignorantia facti.* When it treats of the former type of ignorance it employs the expressions *ignorantia legis*[61] and *ignorantia legum*[62] or *ignorantia circa legem.*[63] *Vermeersch*[64] pointed out that the term *ignorantia iuris* can be used in a two-fold sense: in the more strict usage *ignorantia iuris* signifies ignorance of the *content of the law;* secondly, and in a less strict but proper sense, it refers to ignorance of the *existence* of the law. In the latter case the law is regarded as a fact and consequently *ignorantia iuris* in this sense is regarded as a kind of *ignorance of fact.*

It seems therefore that the legislator chose the phrase *ignorantia circa legem* in preference to the term *ignorantia iuris,* since he also treated ignorance of fact *(ignorantia circa factum)* in the same paragraph of the canon; in this way he intended to prevent any possible ambiguity that might otherwise have arisen.

The second type of ignorance on the basis of the unknown object mentioned in the canon is *ignorance of the penalty.* Ignorance of the penalty *(ignorantia circa poenam)* can be present in two ways: when one does not know that a penalty is attached to the violation of a certain law, or second, when one does not know the particular penalty which is annexed to the commission of a crime.

Ignorance of the penalty and ignorance of fact in the various subdivisions indicated in the canon and also ignorance of the law will be treated separately in a later chapter.

---

[61] Canon 2229, § 1 and § 3, n. 1.

[62] Canon 16, § 1.

[63] Canon 16, § 2.

[64] *Theologia Moralis,* I, 74.

CHAPTER VI

EFFECTS OF IGNORANCE UPON INVALIDATING AND DISQUALIFYING LAWS

General Considerations

Modestinus (fl. ca. 250) classified the four effects of law in his classical statement "legis virtus haec est: imperare, vetare, permittere, punire."[1] The function of law is to command, to forbid, to permit and to punish. Laws are made primarily, proximately and essentially to give rise to a moral obligation which binds in conscience. This obligation derives from the very nature of law and distinguishes laws from counsels, recommendations and warnings.

If laws did not exert a binding force in conscience, subjects would conform to them only when they could not possibly evade the penalty, and such a situation would lead to flagrant hypocrisy and widespread deception among those for whom the laws are made.[2]

Several corollaries necessarily follow from the moral obligation arising from the nature of law. First of all, those who are bound by the law must acquaint themselves with the commands and prohibitions of the legislator, since it is impossible for them to conform to what is not known. Obviously, therefore, they must employ the means requisite for gaining knowledge of the law either by referring to the legal text or by having recourse to one who is informed in regard to the law. It is not demanded, however, that extraordinary means be used. A further obligation requires that all unnecessary proximate occasions of violating the law be avoided; otherwise the law would prove useless.[3]

---

[1] D (1, 3) 7.

[2] Cf. *Summa Theologica*, Ia IIae, q. 90, art. 1; q. 96, a. 4; Schmalzgrueber, *Ius Ecclesiasticum Universum*, lib. I, pars. I, tit. II, n. 30.

[3] Cf. Cocchi, *Commentarium in Codicem Iuris Canonici*, Liber I,

Preceptive laws are those laws which command that an act be placed, such as attending Holy Mass on Sunday and holy days of obligation, or fasting on certain days. These laws oblige *semper et non pro semper,* that is, they bind only at certain times. It is apparent that all preceptive laws of this type could not bind simultaneously, since man is not capable of performing every good action at every given moment.[4]

On the other hand, prohibitive laws oblige *semper et pro semper,* since they forbid the performance either of an evil action or of acts in themselves indifferent which cause some harm to the common good. Both categories of acts are always forbidden.

Some authors classify invalidating and disqualifying laws as prohibitive,[5] while others choose to treat them under a separate category.[6]

The former classification is based on the historical development of the distinction between laws which simply prohibit and laws which both prohibit and invalidate;[7] however, some *prescriptive* laws are invalidating, namely, those which require that a determined *extrinsic* form or certain solemnities or conditions be observed for the validity of acts.[8] Other prescriptive laws provide

---

Normae Generales (3. ed., Taurinorum Augustae: Marietti, 1925), p. 106 (hereafter cited *Normae Generales*); Michael Bargilliat, *Praelectiones Juris Canonici* (37. ed., 2 vols., Parisiis: Apud Baston, Berche et Pagis, 1923), I, n. 86; Vermeersch-Creusen, *Epitome Iuris Canonici,* I, n. 72.

[4] Authors also designate this type of laws as *affirmative,* v. g., Vermeersch-Creusen (*Epitome Iuris Canonici,* I, 73), Cicognani (*Canon Law,* p. 530), and others. Prohibitive laws are called *negative;* cf. *loc. cit.*

[5] Bargilliat, *Praelectiones Juris Canonici,* I, nn. 66-68; Cicognani, *Canon Law,* p. 531.

[6] Cappello, *Summa Iuris Canonici* (3 vols., Vol. I, 4. ed., 1945; Vol. III, 2. ed., 1940, Romae: Apud Aedes Universitatis Gregorianae), I, n. 68; Vermeersch-Creusen, *Epitome Iuris Canonici,* I, n. 76; Beste, *Introductio in Codicem* (3. ed., Collegeville, Minn.: St. John's Abbey Press, 1946), p. 68.

[7] Pichler, *Jus Canonicum,* lib. I, tit. II, nn. 70-71; Reiffenstuel, *Jus Canonicum Universum,* lib. I, tit. II, n. 244; *op. cit.,* cap. II, ad Reg. 64, R. J., in VI°; Schmalzgrueber, *Ius Ecclesiasticum Universum,* lib. I, tit. II, n. 5.

[8] Canon 1680, § 1.

that some acts obtain juridical existence only if certain essential constitutive elements are present.[9]

Before the advent of the present Code, extensive consideration was given to the nature and the effects of prohibitive laws. The Roman Law principle that all acts contrary to prohibitive laws were null and void[10] was undoubtedly incorporated into Canon Law.[11] However, Pope Innocent III (1198-1216) distinguished between laws which simply prohibited certain acts and those which contained prohibitions with invalidating effects.[12] Nevertheless, some canonists[13] continued to emphasize the Roman Law principle and considered Pope Innocent's teaching acceptable only within certain limitations, while many others followed the Pontiff's principle.[14] Ultimately the latter opinion supplanted the former in practice and became universally accepted.[15] Thus a clear distinction was drawn between a prohibition as such, and a prohibition to which was joined an invalidating force. Furthermore, the canonists taught that the legislator was obliged to frame the law in such a manner that it could be known when he intended a law to have an invalidating force.[16] These principles applied equally to disqualifying laws.

---

[9] Cf. canon 1680, § 1; canon 488, n. 1; Josephus D'Annibale, *Summula Theologiae Moralis* (5. ed., 3 vols., Romae, 1908), I, n. 211.

[10] "Ea quae lege fieri prohibentur, si fuerint facta, non solum inutilia, sed pro infectis etiam habeantur."—C. (I, 14) 5.

[11] C. 13, C. XXV, q. 2: "Quae contra ius fiunt, debent utique pro infectis haberi."—Pope Gregory I (a. 590-604); Reiffenstuel, *Tractatus de Regulis Juris*, ad. R. J. 64.

[12] C. 16, X, *de regularibus et transeuntibus ad religionem*, III, 31: "multa fieri prohibentur, quae, si facta fuerint, obtinent roboris firmitatem."

[13] Cf. Suarez treats this controversy at length.—*De Legibus*, lib. V, c. 25.

[14] Suarez, *op. cit.*, lib. V., c. 25, praes, n. 21 ss. et c. 29; Reiffenstuel, *Jus Canonicum Universum*, lib. I, tit. II, n. 243 ss.

[15] Cf. D'Annibale, *Summula Theologiae Moralis*, I, n. 210.

[16] Cf. Suarez, *De Legibus*, V, c. 26-27; D'Annibale, *op. cit.*, I, n. 213. This principle was incorporated into canon 11—"Irritantes aut inhabilitantes eae tantum leges habendae sunt, quibus aut actum esse nullum aut inhabilem esse personam *expresse* vel *aequivalenter* statuitur (italics inserted)." Cf. Michiels, *Normae Generales*, I, 103-105; 275-277; Cicognani, *Canon Law*, p. 560.

ARRICLE 1. DEFINITIONS AND DIVISIONS OF INVALIDATING AND DISQUALIFYING LAWS

An invalidating law is a law which renders null and void acts which by the natural law and the general principles of the positive or human law would be otherwise valid. The Latin word *irritare* means *to render null,* that is, of no account, from *reor*—meaning *I decree* or *constitute* and *in,* a negative *particle,* signifying *not.*[17] Disqualifying laws render a person juridically incapable of placing certain acts which of themselves could be performed according to divine positive or natural law. Disqualifying laws directly affect the agent and remove his capacity to act validly; only *indirectly* is the act itself affected.[18] On the other hand, invalidating laws *directly* pertain to the act, depriving it of all juridical force; this may be effected directly, namely, when the law simply states that the act is invalid,[19] or indirectly, when the law prescribes that a form or a solemnity be observed for the valid fulfillment of an act.[20]

1. Kinds of Invalidating and Disqualifying Laws

Invalidating and disqualifying laws in the strict sense are only such laws which render an act invalid or a person disqualified *ipso facto,* so that the act or the person by his action at no time produces any juridic effect.[21]

Certain other laws render actions invalid or persons disqualified from the beginning, but nevertheless require that this invalidity or disqualification be declared by competent authority in order

---

[17] Cf. Toso, *Commentaria Minora,* I, 35. When referring to laws which are invalidating by the natural or divine positive laws, some authors use the expressions *infecti* or *inexistentes,* while they reserve the terms *irriti* and *nulli* to acts which are of their very nature valid, but which are deprived of their juridical effect by the human law; however, this distinction is not adhered to universally—Cf. Vermeersch, *Quaestiones de Justitia* (1 vol., Brugis, 1901), n. 325; A. Van Gestel, *De Justitia et Lege Civili* (Groningae, 1896), c. II, § 4, n. 72 ss.

[18] E. g., canons 968, § 1; 1067, § 1; 1072; 1073; 1076.

[19] Cf. e. g., canon 572, § 1, n. 3.

[20] Cf., v. g., canons 555, § 1; 1017, § 1; 1094.

[21] Cf. canons 150, § 1; 729; 1067 and the following.

that the invalidating or disqualifying effect be recognized in the external forum.[22]

It should be observed that those laws which render acts rescissible in virtue of the action of a judge cannot be called invalidating or disqualifying in the proper sense of the term. In such cases the sentence of the judge does not merely declare a pre-existing invalidity but actually effects it.[23]

On the basis of the purpose for which the legislator established invalidating or disqualifying laws, these laws are divided into those which are *merely* invalidating or disqualifying, i.e., when they have been made directly for the promotion of the common good, such as the legislation relative to the form of marriage[24] and the law regarding the required age for valid perpetual religious profession,[25] and, secondly, into those laws whose invalidating and disqualifying effect is of the nature of a penalty attached to the commission of a crime or a delictual fact; for example, the accomplices in the act of spouse-murder cannot enter a subsequent valid marriage between themselves.[26]

Some canonists,[27] following some pre-Code authors,[28] distinguish between those which are primarily invalidating and secondarily penal, and those which are primarily penal and secondarily invalidating.[29] However, all laws whatsoever which contain invalidating or disqualifying effects are *primarily* directed toward the promotion of the common good or the protection of individuals

---

[22] E.g., canon 2294, § 1; cf. Michiels, *Normae Generales*, I, 269.

[23] Cf. canons 103, § 2; 162, § 2; 1687, § 1. Cf. also Michiels, *Normae Generales*, I, p. 269, note 2.

[24] Canon 1094.

[25] Canon 573.

[26] Canon 1075, n. 3. Cf. canons 2294, § 1; 1072, 1530, § 1, n. 3. Michiels, *op. cit.* I, 271.

[27] Noldin, *Summa Theologiae Moralis*, I, n. 168, n. 4; Maroto, *Institutiones Iuris Canonici*, I, n. 231.

[28] Cf. Suarez, *De Legibus*, lib. V, cap. 22; Sanchez, *De Sancto Matrimonii Sacramento*, lib. III, disp. 17, n. 10 ss; Thomas Bouquillon, *Theologia Moralis Fundamentalis* (2. ed., Brugis, 1890), n. 167.

[29] This distinction is noteworthy, since certain authors use it as the basis for their opinion in regard to the effect of ignorance on invalidating and disqualifying laws. Cf. D'Annibale, *Summula Theologiae Moralis*, I, n. 214, nota 13.

in a special manner, and even though an invalidating or disqualifying effect appears in the law as a penalty, such laws are not to be regarded as essentially or necessarily penal.[30]

2. *Authors of Invalidating and Disqualifying Laws*

It is universally admitted that both civil and ecclesiastical authorities who enjoy legislative power can issue laws which have invalidating and disqualifying effects, since these laws are so vastly conducive to the common good. Consequently these laws may be issued by the following: the Supreme Pontiff, who exercises supreme and complete power of jurisdiction over the Universal Church;[31] an ecumenical council when it is lawfully convoked;[32] plenary and provincial councils within their respective territorial limits;[33] bishops within their own dioceses, whether they issue these laws on the occasion of a synod or outside of it,[34] and provided that they act within the scope of the jurisdiction granted to them by the law;[35] prelates *nullius*, vicars apostolic, prefects apostolic, and administrators apostolic who are permanently appointed;[36] cathedral chapters or diocesan consultors when the see is vacant and provided that a vicar capitular or a diocesan administrator has not yet been elected; vicars capitular or diocesan administrators according to the determinations of law;[37] exempt major

[30] Cf. Michiels, *Normae Generales*, I, p. 363, note 1: ". . . omnis lex irritans est semper primario irritans, ita ut irritatio poenalis numquam considerari possit ut vera poena neque ipsi applicari possint principia circa excusationem a poena statuta (can. 2218, § 2 et can. 2229), sed e contra considerari debeat ut effectus sui generis, a poena prorsus distinctus, ipsique applicari debeant principia specialissima hic, in can. 16, § 1, quoad excusationem statuta." Cf. Beste, *Introductio in Codicem*, p. 69.

[31] Canon 218.

[32] Cf. canon 222, 227, 228.

[33] Cf. canons 290, 291.

[34] Cf. canon 329.

[35] Ordinaries are restricted in regard to attaching diriment and impedient impediments to marriage; cf. canon 1038, 1039, § 2, 1040. They likewise may not annex a further reservation to censures already reserved to the Holy See; cf. canon 2247, § 1.

[36] Cf. canons 293-327.

[37] Cf. canons 429-444.

religious superiors of men religious in unison with general and provincial chapter meetings, in regard to their subjects.[38]

All these ecclesiastical superiors enjoy legislative power in virtue of which they may issue invalidating and disqualifying laws; but in framing these laws they are obliged to mention the invalidating or disqualifying effect in express or equivalent terms.[39]

ARTICLE 2. IGNORANCE AS AN EXCUSE FROM INVALIDATING AND DISQUALIFYING LAWS

Prior to the Code ignorance was admitted as an excuse from certain types of invalidating and disqualifying laws.[40] The authors distinguished between laws which were simply invalidating and disqualifying, and those which were simply invalidating and penal simultaneously. No ignorance whatsoever, even invincible ignorance, excused from the former. However, a distinction was made in regard to the invalidating penal laws, namely, into those laws which were primarily invalidating *(primario irritans)* and only secondarily penal *(secundario penalis),* and into those laws which were primarily penal and only secondarily invalidating. Ignorance did not excuse from the former, but in regard to the latter category the authors held that whatever ignorance excused from morally grave culpability, e.g., invincible ignorance, excused likewise from the invalidating effect.[41]

However, it was disputed whether ignorance which did not excuse from culpability or which only lessened it, namely, ignorance of fact or of the penalty (invalidating), likewise excused from the invalidity. In this regard, Schmalzgrueber (1663-1735),[42] Ballerini (1805-1881)—Palmieri (1829-1909)[43] and others were

---

[38] The moderators general of these institutes are generally not empowered personally to make laws. The laws are usually enacted at the general chapters. Cf. Cicognani, *Canon Law,* p. 533.

[39] Cf. canon 11.

[40] Cf. Saurez, *De Legibus,* lib. V, cap. 22; Sanchez, *De Sancto Matrimonio Sacramento,* lib. III, disp. 17, n. 10 ss; Bouquillon, *Theologia Moralis Fundamentalis,* n. 167.

[41] Cf. *supra.*

[42] *Jus Ecclesiasticum Universum,* lib. V, tit. 37, n. 105.

[43] Antonius Ballerini et Dominicus Palmieri, *Opus Theologicum Morale* (7 vols., Prati, 1889-1893), II, tit. I, nn. 316-317.

of the opinion that ignorance of the invalidity excused from it, since such an extraordinary penalty was equal to the juridical effects of a censure; on the other hand, Suarez, (1548-1617),[44] D'Annibale (1815-1892),[45] the Salmanticenses (1665-1724)[46] and others held the more common opinion that ignorance did not excuse, since ignorance of the penalty alone did not excuse from culpability; furthermore, ignorance did not generally excuse from incurring the penalty attached to the violation of the law, censures excepted.

The Code enunciated the general and absolute principle that no ignorance excuses from the effect of invalidating or disqualifying laws unless the contrary is expressly stated. Consequently, the words *nulla ignorantia* include the following types of ignorance: vincible and invincible, culpable and inculpable, ignorance of law (*mere irritans, mere inhabilitans,* whether prohibitive, preceptive or penal), and, finally, ignorance of fact. Consequently, every act performed in ignorance is null and void; and in like manner, when an agent objectively lacks certain qualities required in order to act validity, ignorance does not excuse him from the disqualifying effects if he acts contrary to the law.

Therefore, if a woman accepts an invitation to marry a man who, unknown to her, is related to her by consanguinity in the third degree of the collateral line, and he, on the other hand, knows of the relationship, but is ignorant of the law of the Church forbidding such marriages under the pain of invalidity, the subsequent marriage is null and void, unless a dispensation has been obtained from the diriment impediment.[47] The juridical effects

---

[44] *De Legibus*, lib. V, c. 22, n. 5 and c. 15, n. 10.

[45] *Summula Theologiae Moralis*, I, n. 216 ss.

[46] *Cursus Theologiae Moralis* (6 vols. in 4, Venetiis, 1714-1728, tract. XI, c. 1, n. 78.

[47] Cf. Chelodi, *Ius Matrimoniale iuxta Codicem Iuris Canonici* (3. ed., Tridenti: Libr. Edit. Tridentum, 1921), n. 114; Cappello, *De Sacramentis*, Vol. III, *De Matrimonio* (2. ed., Romae, 1927), III, n. 589; Blat, *Commentarium Textus Codices Iuris Canonici* (5 vols. in 6, Liber III, *De Sacramentis* (2. ed., Romae, 1924), Liber III, pars I, n. 484 (hereafter cited *De Sacramentis*).

of the law are produced independently of the knowledge or opinion of the contracting parties.[48]

It is worthy of note that the Church sometimes makes concessions to those who contravene invalidating laws in good faith. Thus, when one or both spouses contract a marriage which is invalid because of an impediment of which they are ignorant, the marriage, although invalid, is designated as a putative marriage, and the offspring of such a union is legitimate.[49]

Invalidity and juridical disqualification may follow the performance of an act after the manner of a penalty. Thus canon 1075 treats of the diriment impediment of crime,[50] and canon 1078 considers the diriment impediment of public honesty.[51] However, whenever the legislator annexes an invalidating or a disqualifying clause to a law, even when the validity or disqualification is consequent upon the commission of a crime or a delictual fact, the effect always follows even though the agent acts in ignorance or through neglect. Every type of invalidating or disqualifying legislation is made specifically and primarily for the common good as a necessary and essential means of promoting the public welfare, whether these laws regard canonical elections, marriage contracts, religious profession or other matters. Consequently every act which is null and void by law cannot be considered as valid even though a particular agent may have acted in ignorance or error.

---

[48] Julius De Becker, *De Sponsalibus et Matrimonio Praelectiones Canonicae* (Bruxellis, 1896), p. 60; A. Gougnard, *Tractatus de Matrimonio* (7. ed., Mechliniae, 1931), p. 160.

[49] Cf. canons 1015, § 4, and 1114.

[50] "Valide contrahere nequeunt matrimonium: 1°. Qui, perdurante eodem legitimo matrimonio, adulterium inter se consummarunt et fidem sibi mutuo dederunt de matrimonio ineundo vel ipsum matrimonium, etiam per civilem tantum actum, attentarunt; 2°. Qui, perdurante pariter eodem legitimo matrimonio, adulterium inter se consummarunt eorumque alter coniugicidium patravit; 3°. Qui mutua opera physica vel morali, etiam sine adulterio, mortem coniugi intulerunt."

[51] "Impedimentum publicae honestatis oritur ex matrimonio invalido, sive consummato sive non, et ex publico vel notorio concubinatu; et nuptias dirimit in primo et secundo gradu lineae rectae inter virum et consanguineas mulieris, ac vice versa."

Whenever a fact is the foundation or the proper cause of invalidity or disqualification, that fact must be formally verified in reality, otherwise the effect does not follow. Thus in the diriment impediment of crime, the fact on which the invalid matrimonial contract is founded is a real act of formal consummated adultery accompanied with an express, absolute and mutual promise to marry after the death or disposal of the unwanted partner or partners.[52] Consequently, if one of the parties is inculpably ignorant that the law forbids adultery, or if he does not know that the act which he exercised was the act of adultery forbidden by law, the diriment impediment is not incurred. However, if the parties formally commit an act which is adultery in the strict sense, even though they are ignorant that a diriment impediment will result from their crime, they are nevertheless rendered incapable of contracting a valid marriage with each other.[53]

Cappello gives the following reasons for the institution of this impediment: to safeguard good morals and the dignity of the sacrament; to protect conjugal fidelity so that a spouse accomplice to adultery or spouse-murder cannot carry his designs to completion; finally, to punish the commission of these crimes which heap such flagrant abuse upon matrimony and upon an innocent spouse.[54]

1. Nisi aliud expresse dicatur[55]

Ignorance of invalidating and disqualifying laws excuses only

---

[52] Canon 1075; cf. Ayrinhac-Lydon, *Marriage Legislation in the New Code of Canon Law* (new rev. ed., New York: Benziger Bros., 1932), pp. 163-164.

[53] Cf. Cappello, *Tractatus Canonico-Moralis de Sacramentis*, Vol. V, *De Matrimonio* (5 ed., Romae: Marietti, 1947), nn. 480-482 (hereafter cited *De Matrimonio*).

[54] *Op cit.*, n. 499; cf. also p. 471, notes 67 and 68. Ioannes Chelodi, *Ius Canonicum de Matrimonio* (5. ed., a Pio Cipratti, Vicenza: Società Anonima Tipografica Editrice, 1947), n. 92: "Licet impedimentum redundet etiam in poenam, natura sua et praecipue est *inhabilitas* personalis, et cavet *honestati* morum atque *dignitati* sacramenti. Unde sequitur nullam ignorantiam ab eo incurrendo excusare."

[55] Canon 16, § 1: Nulla ignorantia legum irritantium aut inhabili-

when an *express* exception or provision is made in the law. A provision or exception can be expressed by the law in two ways: explicitly or implicity.

1. A provision or exception is *explicitly* established only when the legislator manifests his will distinctly and in language the natural meaning of which establishes the exception without any necessity of recurring to a discursive process.

2. *Implicitly,* when the provision or exception is not distinctly formulated in the law, but is drawn from the law as an immediate and necessary conclusion.[56]

The following canons point out what is required first of all for the valid performance of certain acts, and secondly, how the law expressly provides for ignorance in certain instances. Thus, in order to hear confessions validly, the law requires that a validly ordained priest have ordinary or expressly delegated jurisdiction,[57] which may be further circumscribed within certain limits.[58] Moreover, in order to hear the confessions of women religious, a confessor needs special jurisdiction, which is obtained only from the local ordinary of the place where the religious house is located.[59]

However, it may happen that when a confessor has received jurisdiction for a definite period, he will through inadvertence absolve a penitent after the time has elapsed; or in another instance a confessor whose faculties are restricted to a limited number of cases may through inadvertence grant absolution beyond the number of cases specified in his faculties. In these two instances the law expressly states that the Church supplies the requisite jurisdiction,and the absolutions, therefore, are valid.[60]

The Church also supplies jurisdiction in the case of common error.[61] Likewise, if a confessor in ignorance absolves from a

---

tantium ab eisdem excusat, *nisi aliud expresse dicatur.* (Italics are the writer's.)

[56] Michiels, *Normae Generales,* I, 103-105; 365; Vermeersch-Cruesen, *Epitome Iuris Canonici,* I, n. 56.

[57] Canons 872; 879, § 1.

[58] Canon 878, § 1.

[59] Canon 876.

[60] Canon 207, § 2.

[61] Canon 209; cf. James Kelly, *The Jurisdiction of the Simple Confessor* (New York: Benziger Bros., 1929), pp. 119-141.

reserved censure, the absolution is valid unless the censure is a censure reserved *specialissimo modo* to the Holy See or a censure which has derived *ab homine*.[62] The absolutions are valid even if the confessor acts in crass or supine ignorance.[63]

2. *Irregularities*

Canon 988, which states: "Ignorantia irregularitatum sive ex delicto sive ex defectu atque impedimentorum ab eisdem non excusat," is in a certain sense an application of the principle of canon 16, § 1. Canon 988 differs from canon 16, § 1, inasmuch as irregularities and impediments refer not to the *valid* but to the *licit* reception or exercise of Holy Orders.[64] However, the purposes of invalidating laws and irregularities are similar in so far as the latter are directly and primarily established by the lawgiver in order to foster and protect the dignity of the clerical state.[65] Furthermore, irregularities and impediments to Holy Orders are not primarily punishments.[66]

Irregularities which arise from the commission of a delict are not incurred by a person who acts bona fide. A formal mortal sin must be committed. Consequently, whenever ignorance, error or inadvertence influence an objectively grave act so as to change its moral character from mortal to venial, the irregularity *ex delicto* does not follow; however, ignorance of the irregularity as such never excuses.

---

[62] Canon 2247, § 3; S.C.S. Off., 11 maii 1892—*Fontes*, n. 1154.

[63] Cf. Cappello, *De Censuris iuxta Codicem Iuris Canonici* (3. ed., Taurinorum Augustae: Marietti, 1933), n. 73.

[64] Cf. canons 984 and 985.

[65] P. Gasparri, *Tractatus de Sacra Ordinatione* (2 vols., Parisiis, 1893), II, tit. I, n. 170 et n. 203 ss.

[66] Cf. Cappello, *Tractatus Canonico-moralis de Sacramentis*, Vol. IV, *De Ordine* (2. ed., Romae: Marietti, 1947), nn. 435-448 (hereafter cited *De Ordine*).

CHAPTER VII

CANON 16, § 2

Ignorantia vel error circa legem aut poenam aut circa factum proprium aut circa factum alienum notorium generatim non praesumitur; circa factum alienum non notorium praesumitur, donec contrarium probetur.

The entire second paragraph of canon 16 will be treated in this chapter. The first point to be studied will concern the nature and the kinds of presumptions. This will be followed by a consideration of the ways by which presumptions can be overthrown, especially the presumptions regarding ignorance. In view of the fact that the major portion of this work is concerned with the presumptions contained in canon 16, § 2, particular emphasis will be placed upon presumptions of law, i.e., of the type *"iuris simpliciter."* The articles devoted to the nature and kinds of presumptions and the article treating the presentation of contrary proof will be followed by single articles treating the separate legal presumptions contained in the canon. The material will be presented according to the order in which the presumptions are mentioned in the Code, with the exception of the article regarding contrary proofs. It is imperative to consider canon 2202, § 2, in relation to this study. Consequently this point will be treated in a separate article, which follows the consideration of the presumption regarding ignorance of the penalty.

ARTICLE 1. THE NATURE OF PRESUMPTIONS

An etymological analysis of the word "presumption" shows that it is derived from the Latin *"prae"* meaning "before," and *"sumere"* meaning "to accept," that is, to accept something as the truth before a demonstration is advanced.[1] A presumption

---

[1] Cf. Schmalzgrueber, *Ius Ecclesiasticum Universum*, lib. IV, tit. XXIII, § 1, n. 1. Regatillo, *Institutiones Iuris Canonici* (2 vols., Santander: Sal Terrae; Vol. I, 2 ed., 1946; Vol. II, 1942), II, 234.

is a probable judgment or a reasonable conclusion made in doubtful matters and based on evidence which is certainly known, and which is intimately connected with the actual truth of the matter. Canon 1825, § 1 states: "Praesumptio est rei incertae probabilis coniectura; eaque alia est iuris, quae ab ipsa lege statuitur; alia hominis quae a iudice coniicitur." A presumption is of the nature of an inference made in doubtful matters for the purpose of establishing the truth.

According to the study of logic an inference is a conclusion drawn from two propositions or facts. Frequently conclusions are drawn from a single proposition or fact without a proper advertence to the process of thought. Furthermore, in order to have a sound deduction, the foundation for the deduction, whether it is a fact or a proposition, must be known or assumed to be true, established or recognized as such in ordinary life. If this is lacking, the deduction is certainly unwarranted.

The canon quoted above describes a presumption as a *"probabilis coniectura."* A presumption is not equal to an absolute certainty; it is a qualified judgment made in uncertain matters. The word *"probabilis"* is used, for a conjecture may prove to be false.[2] Likelihood is one of the essential qualities of a presumption, since the opposite may be true.[3] A presumption is called a *probable conjecture* since it is based on what *ordinarily* happens according to the common practice.[4]

Although a person who makes a presumption does not have absolute certitude, nevertheless he must base his opinion on signs or indications which strengthen his opinion with a foundation or

---

[2] Michiels, *Normae Generales*, I, 339: "Sunt tamen casus, in quibus *factum a lege revera existere praesumitur* et ut revera existens ordinatur, quin de reali facti veritate seu existentia in casu concreto curetur."

[3] Cf. s. D'Angelo, *Ius Digestorum* (2 vols., Romae, 1927-1928), I, 488; John Henry Card. Newman, *Grammar of Assent* (Longmans, Green & Co., 1903), p. 60.

[4] Michiels, *op. cit.*, I, 339-340: "In his casibus scilicet legislator, ex eo quod factum aliquod juxta notum communem hominum agendi morem in determinatis circumstantiis *ordinarie* contingit, in iisdem circumstantiis *semper* contingere legitime praesumit" (italcis inserted).

reason, as in cause and effect. The inference he makes should be in proportion to the force of the indications or signs. The foundations, therefore, are described as signs, circumstances, *"indicia,"* arguments, suspicions, adminicles, or, in short, facts, indications, or circumstances.[5]

Judicial matters always involve human affairs, and in such affairs no more than moral certitude can be obtained. This certitude is distinct from the two other types of certitude, namely, metaphysical and physical, which philosophers treat of. Of the three, moral certitude is the weakest, although it is the one that governs all human relations. It is based on the word or experience of another which one is made aware of, or it may spring from personal experience or experience with others.[6]

The facts, the signs, the circumstances and the indications are the starting point in a presumption. They may be defined as "any significant mark which aids one in discovering the truth of doubtful events."[7]

Authors in analysing the relationship between the foundations of the presumption and the presumption itself divide the former into slight and grave indications.[8] These classifications of *"indicia"* give rise to presumptions that are either light or strong or violent according to the accepted terminology.[9]

---

[5] Udalricus Beste, *Introductio in Codicem* (3. ed., Collegeville, Minn.: Saint John's Abbey Press, 1946), p. 826: "Nomen ipsum 'praesumptio,' anglice presumption, circumstantial evidence, definitionem Codicis suggerit, quia aliquid prae-sumere est illud pro vero assumere quin demonstretur."

[6] Cf. Peter Coffey, *The Science of Logic* (2nd impression, 2 vols., London-New York: Longmans, Green & Co., 1918), II, 214.

[7] Schmalzgrueber, *Jus Ecclesiasticum Universum,* lib. IV, tit. XXIII, § 1, n. 20; Menochius, *De Praesumptionibus, Coniecturis, Signis, et Indiciis Commentaria* (2 vols., Coloniae Allobrogum, 1686), lib. I, praesumpt. VII, n. 20 (hereafter cited *De Praesumptionibus*); Hinchius, *Kirchenrecht,* VI, 106.

[8] Cf. Schmalzgrueber, *Jus Ecclesiasticum Universum,* lib. IV, tit. XXIII, § 1, n. 20; Reiffenstuel, *Jus Canonicum Universum,* lib. II, tit. 23, § 1, n. 15; Cocchi, *Commentarium in Codicem Iuris Canonici,* Liber IV, *De Processibus* (3. ed., Taurinorum Augustae: Marietti, 1940), lib. IV, nn. 181-184 (hereafter cited *De Processibus*).

[9] Cf. Felix Cappello, *Summa Iuris Canonici* (3 vols., Vol. III, 2. ed.,

ARTICLE 2. PRESUMPTIONS OF MAN

A *"presumptio hominis"* may be defined as a conjecture not expressed in or based on the law, but drawn from circumstances of the case and accepted as true until the contrary is demonstrated.[10] A legal presumption has for its origin the law itself, whereas a presumption of man is one which a judge or a prudent person forms for himself. It is solely the product of the human mind. The person bases his conjecture upon the normal mode of action for human beings. The deduction, however, is colored and limited by the judge's understanding of the circumstances of the case and his personal evaluation of the indications present.

Canon 1828 states, however, that these presumptions are not to be conjectured by the judge except from a certain and specific fact which is directly connected with the matter in controversy. The presumption as a conclusion must follow from a specific fact established by evidence in the case. The Code thus restricts the use of presumptions, since all inferential evidence is dangerous and can easily mislead.

The judge or the prudent person must have moral certainty before he arrives at his conjecture. The degree of moral certitude depends upon the nature of the grounds on which the presumption is based. The degrees of value which presumptions enjoy are not merely arbitrary; experience and the customs of nations and the norms which influence the estimation of human conduct determine their weight.[11]

These presumptions can be overthrown even though the inferences are valid and based on universals that lead to moral certainty.[12] The only conclusive way to overcome a presumption is to establish the truth; however, other contrary presumptions

---

Romae: Apud Aedis Universitatis Gregorianae, 1940), III, n. 219; Wernz, *Ius Decretalium* (2 ed., 6 vols., Romae et Prati, 1906-1913), V. n. 655; Schmalzgrueber, *Jus Ecclesiasticum Universum*, lib. II, tit. 23, n. 10 s.

[10] Schmalzgrueber, *Jus Ecclesiasticum Universum*, lib. III, tit. 23, § 1, n. 4; Cappello, *Summa Iuris Canonici*, III, n. 219.

[11] Cicognani, *Canon Law*, p. 626.

[12] Beste, *Introductio in Codicem*, p. 826; Noldin-Schmitt, *Summa Theologiae Moralis*, I, 170.

either of the law *(praesumptiones iuris)* or of man *(praesumptiones hominis)* can be set up and can successfully overthrow those that have been made. It is left to the prudence of the judge to estimate the value of presumptions which militate one against the other.

ARTICLE 3. PRESUMPTIONS OF LAW

A *"praesumptio iuris"* is one made by the law itself. These presumptions are drawn by the legislator, whereas presumptions of man are drawn by the judge.[13] In themselves presumptions of danger are considered as relating either to a *private,* that is, a personal danger, or to a *common* danger, according as the law presumes that in certain instances there exists for a particular individual or for everyone a danger of some sort.[14] In such instances the legislator accepts the probable result as it derives from events which are frequent in their occurrence. In setting up these presumptions the legislator is guided by what results from certain facts or circumstances in the generality of cases.[15]

Presumptions of law concern future acts and are limited in number and conditions by the law itself; presumptions of man are made in respect to past acts and are unlimited in number.

The foundation of a presumption of law is some abstract situation which may be a fact or a collection of facts or circumstances.[16] Whenever this abstract situation or collection of facts materializes

---

[13] Canon 1825, § 2, distinguishes between two kinds of presumptions of law: "Praesumptio iuris alia est iuris simpliciter, alia iuris et de iure." The latter, *iuris et de iure,* is an absolute presumption which admits of only indirect proof to the contrary (canon 1826), e.g., canon 1904 establishes an absolute presumption in favor of a juridical sentence which has become a *res iudicata.* The legal presumption in canon 16, § 2, is *iuris simplicter,* and can be overcome directly or indirectly (canon 1826).

[14] Cicognani, *Canon Law,* p. 626.

[15] Cf. Michiels, *Normae Generales,* I, 340.

[16] Cf. Michiels, *Normae Generales,* I, 339-343. It is patent that presumptions are widely different from *legal fictions,* although the effects produced by either may be the same. In a fiction of law something is regarded as true although the very contrary is certain. Cf. Reiffenstuel, *Jus Canonicum Universum,* lib. I, tit. II, nn. 176-196; Michiels, *op. cit.,* I, 342; Cocchi, *Normae Generales,* I, 109.

in a certain case, the law itself states the outcome. But these laws do not apply in some cases; the conclusion does not always result as set forth in the presumption. These exceptions do not hinder the existence or the effectiveness of the laws themselves. These exceptions, however, must be demonstrated conclusively and without doubt; otherwise the presumption indicated by law is considered to be verified in the concrete case.[17]

The law directs the judge to abide by these conclusions unless the adversary can prove either directly or indirectly that the presumption does not hold.[18]

Canon 16, § 2, contains the five following presumptions of law:

1. Ignorantia vel error *circa legem* generatim non praesumitur.
2. Ignorantia vel error *circa poenam* generatim non praesumitur.
3. Ignorantia vel error *circa factum proprium* generatim non praesumitur.
4. Ignorantia vel error *circa factum alienum notorium* generatim non paesumitur.
5. Ignorantia vel error *circa factum alienum non notorium* praesumitur.

The first four are negative statements; the fifth is positive. The first two concern ignorance of law; ignorance of the penalty is practically equivalent to ignorance of law. The latter three regard ignorance of fact. The first four are general presumptions; the word *generatim* appears in each statement. The fifth is expressed with relative absoluteness, *"donec contrarium probetur."*

A presumption is a probable conjecture that an uncertain thing exists.[19] The "uncertain thing" in the first four presumptions enumerated in the second paragraph of canon 16 is the *absence of ignorance,* whereas *ignorance* itself is the "uncertain thing" in the final presumption listed in the canon. The phrase *ignorantia . . . non praesumitur* is a purely negative statement which means that *no probable conjecture is established in the law, and that neither may a person in authority, as long as the opposite is not proved, presume* that ignorance exists in the cases mentioned in the law, i.e., in the canon.

---

[17] Michiels, *Normae Generales,* I, 339-340.

[18] Cf. canons 1826 and 1827.

[19] Cf. canon 1825.

It should be noted that the canon does not directly state that knowledge is presumed, i.e., *scientia praesumitur.* Words like *scientia, debita cognitio, scire* or *cognoscere* do not appear in the legal text. In the phrase *scientia praesumitur* two positive terms are used to express the presumption, whereas *ignorantia non praesumitur* contains two negative terms.

From the philosophical approach, does the phrase *ignorantia non praesumitur* mean the same thing as *scientia praesumitur?*

First of all, according to the process of obversion in the science of logic, these two propositions are equivalents. Obversion is the process of substituting for an affirmative proposition its equivalent in negative form. It is asserting the same thing in opposite quality.[20]

Furthermore, ignorance in the strict sense is so entirely negative a thing, that any recession from it whatsoever must be filled with some positive state of mind. Any positive state of mind, however hesitant or fluctuating, can, in at least some analagous sense, be called *scientia.* It may be *scientia dubia* or *haesitans,* but it is *scientia.* Therefore, the phrase *ignorantia non praesumitur* at least implies that *scientia dubia* or *haesitans praesumitur.* However, it would be absurd to maintain that the legislator in constructing the presumptions of canon 16, § 2, intended to regard his subjects as possessing merely some of the variant degrees of knowledge which are found in opinion or doubt or in any other similar state of mind. Obviously, then, the legislator in setting up a legal presumption in regard to the law postulates that the subjects know of the existence, the meaning, and the scope of the law; it can hardly be imagined that he wishes to regard them as possessing merely a doubtful or fluctuating mental attitude toward those rules which they are bound to observe, and which he has duly promulgated in order to promote the common welfare of the society. Indeed, the phrase *ignorantia non praesumitur* has been traditionally understood as an equivalent of *scientia praesumitur.*[21]

---

[20] Cf. J. E. Creighton and H. R. Smart, *Introductory Logic* (5. ed., New York: Macmillan Co., 1932), p. 123.

[21] Cf. C. (1, 14) 9; Ioannes Teutonicus, *Glossa Ordinaria,* ad c. 2, D. LXXXII s.v. *non probatur*; Ioannes Andreae, *Glossa* ad c. 2,

Finally, when the legislator states *ignorantia non praesumitur* he means two things:

1. If anyone is ignorant of certain facts concerning which the law denies the presumption of ignorance, the one who alleges that he did not know must offer positive proof that ignorance did actually exist.

2. Since such an individual must offer positive proof that ignorance existed, it immediately follows that the law presumes that *scientia* does exist until the contrary is proved.

Therefore, if a person is being charged with the violation of law, is threatened with a penalty, is being held responsible for some act which he performed himself, or is being held responsible for the implications in a notorious act performed by someone else, this person is not presumed to have been ignorant. Consequently, if he wishes to offer ignorance as a defense, the burden of proof rests upon him, that is, he must offer positive proof that ignorance did actually exist. Furthermore, since he is thus obliged to offer positive proof that ignorance existed, it follows that the law presumes that *scientia* does exist until the opposite is proved true. Therefore, his position is the same as it would be if the law read *scientia praesumitur.*

Consequently, the phrase *ignorantia non praesumitur* is equivalent to the phrase *scientia praesumitur.*

ARTICLE 4. PROOF OF IGNORANCE

Prior to the presentation of contrary proofs, a presumption of law is maintained as the truth, and in effect constitutes full proof.[22] Furthermore, whenever the foundations for the presumptions are

---

de temporibus ordinationum et qualitate ordinandorum, I, 9, in VI°, s.v. *scienter*: ". . . quod praesumitur sciens, nisi probet ignorantiam"; *Glossa* ad c. 2, *de constitutionibus*, I, 2, in VI°, s.v. *statuta*; Ojetti, *Commentarium in Codicem Iuris Canonici*, I, p. 131, n. 9: ". . . haec autem non praesumitur . . . Imo, argumento a contrario ducto, potius scientia in casu praesumenda est." Cf. also Wernz-Vidal, *Ius Canonicum*, V, 547; Aryhinac-Lydon, *Marriage Legislation*, p. 194; S.C.C., June 15 and May 19, 1889, in *Acta Sanctae Sedis* (41 vols., Romae, 1865-1908), XXI (1889), 180 (hereafter cited *ASS*).

[22] Cf. canon 1747, n. 2.

demonstrated,[23] the presumptions of law become automatically present; thus, when a fact is shown to be notorious, the presumption automatically follows that it is known.[24] Although the law places so much emphasis on the effect of presumptions, it does not consider them evident truth. They always remain deductions based on certain facts or indications. It is evident that whenever the real truth can be shown to be identical with the presumption, then there is regarded as present, not merely a presumption, but the truth of the matter itself. Consequently, every presumption can be overcome by the presentation of evident truth to the contrary.

The law directs the judge to abide by the presumptions of law unless the adversary can prove either directly or indirectly that the presumption does not hold.[25]

The adversary can overcome a presumption of law *directly* by showing that the evident truth is contrary to the presumption, even though the foundation for the presumption does exist. The presumption is overcome *indirectly* when it is shown that the foundation for the presumption does not exist or is lacking in one of its constitutive parts to form a real foundation as required by the presumption.[26] However, if neither of these proofs is adequate to produce moral certainty[27] in the mind of the judge *(probatio plena),*[28] the presumption will be adhered to by the law.[29]

The presumptions as stated in canon 16, § 2, are simple presumptions of law, and consequently, according to canon 1826,

---

[23] Cappello, *Summa Iuris Canonici,* III, n. 220: "Ut quis gaudeat beneficio praesumptionibus iuris, sufficit ut probet facta quibus eadem nititur."

[24] Note, however, that canon 1747 states that notorious facts as understood by the definitions in canon 2197, nn. 2 and 3, do not have to be proved.

[25] Cf. canons 1826-1827.

[26] Canon 1826.

[27] Cf. Pius XII, allocutio, die 1 oct. 1942—*AAS,* XXXIV (1942), 338 ff.

[28] Cf. Cappello, *Summa Iuris Canonici,* III, n. 169; Beste, *Introductio in Codicem,* p. 186.

[29] Canon 1827: "qua non probante, sententia ferri debet in favorem pro qua stat praesumptio."

can be challenged in two days: *directly,* through an examination of the fact which is presumed, and *indirectly,* through an examination of the fact which serves as the basis for the presumption. In the first four presumptions listed in canon 16, § 2, the *res incerta* which is presumed is the *absence of ignorance,* i.e., the presence of knowledge; the *res incerta* of the final presumption listed in the canon (regarding *facta aliena non notoria*) is *ignorance.*[30]

These presumptions one can challenge *directly* by placing on the witness stand the person who pleads ignorance and there subjecting his state of mind to scrutiny. However, it should be observed that since ignorance is a negative state of mind, that is, something of an internal character which cannot be seen or measured physically, it can scarcely be demonstrated by direct proof. Consequently, the person who pleads ignorance can at best establish his allegation *indirectly,* namely, by discounting the fact or circumstance which serves as the basis for the presumption, i.e., by showing that those factors which normally contribute to *ignorance* are verified in his case. Such, for example, would be a lack of instruction, an environment which furnishes a person, not with knowledge, but with misinformation, an absence from the territory since the time the law was promulgated, a temporary condition of insanity, an affliction with grave illness, etc.

Reiffenstuel, in repeating the constant teaching of the canonists,[31] stated the three ways by which ignorance could be proved. First, one could establish it by means of an oath; secondly, by proving a fact, such as insanity, madness, etc., from which it necessarily follows that a person was ignorant; thirdly, by proving a fact, such as absence from a place, which fact not necessarily, indeed, but nevertheless in all likelihood gave rise to ignorance.[32]

---

[30] In some civil law codes knowledge is presumed by an absolute presumption (*praesumption iuris et de iure*). Cf. Cicognani, *Canon Law,* p. 595; Michiels, *Normae Generales,* I, 355, note 1.

[31] *Glossa* ad c. 24, C. XII, q. 2, s. v. *ignorare*; *Glossa* ad c. 6, C. XXXVIII, q. 1, s. v. *probare*; *Glossa* ad c. 6, X, *qui matrimonium accusare possunt, vel contra illud testari,* IV, 18, s. v. *iuramento*; *Glossa* ad c. 2, *de temporibus ordinationum et qualitate ordinandorum,* I, 9, in VI°, s. v. *scienter.*

[32] *Tractatus de Regulis Juris,* ad R.J. 47 in VI°, n. 9: ". . . potest

Consequently the presumption of knowledge can be challenged and vanquished by means of contravening external evidence, by way of contrary presumptions and conjectures, and through a declaratory oath of contradiction.[33] Thus a person by presenting evidence to the effect that he had not been in a territory since the time a law was promulgated can defeat the presumption that he was ignorant of a law or of the penalty attached to the law. Likewise, a person by proving that he was insane can overcome the presumption that he was not ignorant of certain past acts. In another instance, if the defendant shows that one of his past acts was actually of small import, or if he proves that he was beset with grave difficulties and implicated in many distracting affairs at the time, the judge can, by means of a personal presumption—a *praesumptio hominis*—deduce from such facts that he was ignorant of the matters in question;[34] furthermore, he could strengthen his plea and his proof by taking an oath in support of his allegation of ignorance.[35]

A judge, however, would be inclined to regard ignorance of the *facta aliena notoria* as supine ignorance, especially when no diligence was required in order to gain knowledge of the fact.[36] Likewise, a judge will ordinarily regard a lack of knowledge of

---

eam probare triplici modo . . . et quidem primo, medio juramenti . . . probando id ex quo necessario sequitur te ignorasse, v.g., quia fuisti tunc furiosus, phreneticus . . . Tertio, probando id, ex quo non quidem necessario, attamen verisimiliter sequitur, te ignorasse, puta quia fuisti absens."

[33] Cf. Cappello, *Summa Iuris Canonici*, III, n. 220; J. Montes, "La ignorancia en el derecho penal," *Ciudad de Deos*, CXLIX (1927), 55-60; S.R.R., *Vladislavien.* (nullitatis matrimonii), 16 mart. 1920, coram R.P.D. Ioanne Prior, dec. VIII, n. 6—*S. Romanae Rotae Decisiones seu Sententiae* (ab anno 1909) (Romae, 1912-), XII (1920), 56 (hereafter cited *S.R.R. Dec.*).

[34] Cf. Michiels, *Normae Generales*, I, 354.

[35] Cf. canons 1829-1830. The supplementary oath is used whenever there is *incomplete* proof. Authors generally restrict the allowable use of this oath exclusively to *civil* cases. For further consideration, cf. Swoboda, *Ignorance in Relation to the Imputability of Delicts*, p. 188, note 103.

[36] Reiffenstuel, *Tractatus de Regulis Juris*, R.J. 13 in VI°, n. 19; Michiels, *Normae Generales*, I, 354.

matters which pertain to one's office or station as supine ignorance.[37] Furthermore, inadvertence or forgetfulness which is admitted or proved is not equal to a plea of ignorance or error. Inadvertence is momentary ignorance of something which is habitually known,[38] and consequently the presumptions mentioned in canon 16, § 2, as favoring knowledge of law and fact operate more forcibly against the person who alleges inadvertence than against the person who pleads ignorance or error, for when it is admitted or proved that the law or the fact was known, it must likewise be assumed that the person possessed knowledge of the law or the fact when he acted. The burden of the proof rests with the accused.[39]

The last presumption mentioned in canon 16, § 2, states that ignorance of the *facta aliena non notoria* is presumed. The uncertain thing *(res incerta)* which is presumed is *ignorance,* i.e., a lack of knowledge.

This simple presumption of law can be vanquished *directly* through proof that knowledge was possessed by the person in whose favor the presumption stands, or *indirectly* through a subverting of the foundations on which the presumption rests. The presumption can be defeated *directly* through the immediate examination of the party himself, through the testimony of witnesses, or by means of documentary evidence which reveals the mental state of the party; *indirectly,* through proof that the person was actually present when the fact took place, in which event he is presumed to have the knowledge.[40] In another instance this can be accomplished by means of a demonstration that the fact was not of a strictly occult nature[41] and, furthermore, should have been known to the person by reason of his office, position, responsibility, etc. In view of these considerations the person would be

---

[37] Reiffenstuel, *op cit.* R.J. 47 in VI°, n. 10.

[38] Vermeersch, *Theologia Moralis,* I, 72.

[39] Cf. Swoboda, *op. cit.,* p. 169.

[40] Cf. Mascardus, *De Probationibus,* Vol. II, concl. 879, n. 35.

[41] Canonists never required that anyone have knowledge of occult facts pertaining to others. Cf. Hostiensis, *Commentaria,* ad c. 1, X, *de postulatione praelatorum,* I, 5 in lib. I, tit. 4, c. 1, n. 21; Mascardus, *De Probationibus,* Vol. II, concl. 879, n. 15; and others.

presumed to have known such a fact, and consequently, whereas he was antecedently favored with the presumption of ignorance, he is now under the burden of proving that he was ignorant.

ARTICLE 5. IGNORANCE OF THE LAW

Canon 16, § 2, contains the most general presumptions of law in regard to ignorance. The first listed presumption vindicates the rule that ignorance of the law is not presumed.

The legislator presumes that the law is known for the following reasons: first, law is an effective norm in that it imposes an obligation on those for whom it is intended; secondly, law is a publicly announced norm of action which determines the manner in which men are to conduct themselves as members of a society; thirdly, after promulgation has taken place, knowledge of the law can be gained most easily.[42] Finally, since the law is generally known, it is presumed to be known by all. In this regard the following rule is applicable: "Inspicimus in obscuris quod est verisimilius, vel quod plerumque fieri consuevit."[43]

Therefore, from the time that laws have been made and duly promulgated, it must be assumed in the external forum that all those for whom they are intended are aware of them, since they have an obligation to observe them, and obligations must be known before they can be fulfilled.[44]

It should not be inferred from this presumption that the legislator expects his subjects to continue at all times in complete awareness of a detailed legal system. Such an obligation would connote an impossible burden. The legislator does not expect everyone to become a specialist in the law of the Church, nor

---

[42] Reiffenstuel, *Tractatus de Regulis Juris*, ad R. J. 13 in VI°, n. 9—". . . scire, et scire debere facileque posse in iure paria habentur." Cf. D. (17, 2) 51; D. (47, 10) (15, 36).

[43] Reg. 45, R. J. in VI°; cf. Cicognani, *Canon Law*, p. 594.

[44] Cf. Ojetti, *Commentarium in Codicem Iuris Canonici*, I, p. 131, n. 9: ". . . dex rite lata et promulgata obligat subditos ad sui cognitionem, ignorare dispositionem legis est culpa; haec autem non praesumitur, ut merito iam advertebat Ulpianus (D. [1, 14] 9. *Imo, argumento a contrario ducto, potius scientia in casu praesumenda est.*" Cf. also E. Regatillo, *Institutiones Iuris Canonici*, I, 66; C. (1, 14) 9.

does he intend that his subjects be instructed in the Fourth Book of the Code. However, the lawgiver presumes that his subjects are not ignorant of the laws which pertain to them in particular; and, furthermore, he demands that an individual in placing an act or a series of acts be aware of the lawfulness of his action. In stating this presumption of law, the legislator supposes that his subjects have not failed in their obligation.[45]

The interpretation of this presumption of law is derived from the approved authors before the Code, for it can scarcely be admitted that the Code abrogated the commonly accepted and traditional principles in this regard.[46]

The definition of ignorance of the law has been given in the former chapter; the relation between ignorance and error has also been presented. The next question is: at precisely what time does the legislator presume that his subjects know his laws? Law is a public norm of action which the lawgiver or one of his delegates draws up and officially announces in order to foster the common welfare of the society which he governs. The means which he takes in order to make his mind and will known, and thereby to acquaint his subjects with their obligation to act according to a particular mode of action, is called promulgation.[47] The legislator announces his laws publicly in order that the members of the society may both learn of and conform to his legislation.[48]

Promulgation may be defined as the publication of the announcement of law made to the community in the name and authority of the legislator.[49] A legislator promulgates his laws properly when he presents them to the community and in such a public

---

[45] Cf. Menochius, *De Praesumptionibus*, lib. VI, praesumpt. XXIII, nn. 10-12; lib. II, praesumpt. III, n. 1; Reiffenstuel, *Tractatus* de *Regulis Juris*, ad R. J. 13 in VI°, nn. 14, 17.

[46] Cf. Josephus Brys, *Juris Canonici Compendium*, Vol. 1 (Brugis: Desclée de Brouwer et Sii, 1947), p. 127; Michiels, *Normae Generales*, I, 353.

[47] Etymologically the word *promulgation* is derived from the Latin *provulgare—pro* meaning (to place) before, and *vulgare* meaning to make known to all. Cf. O. Mueller, *Sexti Pompeii Festi de Verborum Significatione quae supersunt* (Lipsiae, 1839), p. 224.

[48] Cf. Wernz-Vidal, *Ius Canonicum*, I, 186.

[49] Cappello, *Summa Iuris Canonici*, I, n. 70.

manner that the subjects can gain knowledge of them. Laws are officially presented to the community as such, and only indirectly to the individual members of the community.[50] As members of society with social obligations, individuals are bound to acquaint themselves with the prescriptions or prohibitions of the lawgiver. It is patent that the head of a community could hardly be expected to issue separate notices to each and every individual whom he intends to bind.[51]

Canon 8, § 1, states that laws are instituted when they are promulgated. It is through promulgation that they become effective as rules of conduct which the subjects are obliged to adhere to. Laws do not bind prior to this public and authentic manifestation, since the will of the legislator has not as yet been made known.

Laws are established when they are officially manifested or publicly made known as such to the community for the first time, i.e., when they are promulgated. At that moment there is inherent in the nature of the law itself an *active* obligation, or a force which elicits a *passive* obligation or a mandatory conformity to the law on the part of the community. The active obligation exists formally in the law as such; the passive obligation to observe the law exists in the subject.

The passive obligation is a necessary objective result of law, even though individual subjects may not actually know of the law; however, as soon as the subjects become aware of the law, this obligation becomes formal and subjective. The *passive* obligation in the former instance may be designated as existing *in actu primo,* and in the latter case as existing *in actu secundo.*[52]

The active obligation and the passive obligation as existing *in actu primo* become simultaneously effective through the act of promulgation,[53] and subsequently, when the subject becomes aware

[50] Michiels, *Normae Generales,* I, 149.

[51] Vermeersch-Creusen, *Epitome Iuris Canonici,* I, n. 65. *Divulgation* of law denotes any act or means whereby the members of a community come to the knowledge of laws which have been already promulgated.—Beste, *Introductio in Codicem,* p. 63.

[52] Cf. M. J. Lohmuller, *The Promulgation of Law,* The Catholic University of American Canon Law Studies, n. 241 (Washington, D. C.: The Catholic University of America Press, 1947), pp. 10 ff.

[53] Cf. Panormitanus, *Commentaria in Quinque Libros Decretalium* in

of the law, he is further bound *in actu secundo*. The latter obligation comes into effect at the moment the individual actually possesses knowledge of the law.

When precisely, however, does the legislator presume that the law is known?

1. Whenever a *vacatio legis* is granted, the law is presumed to be known at the conclusion of the *vacatio*. A *vacatio legis* is a period of time following the promulgation, during which period the subjects are not bound *in actu secundo* to observe the laws. Thus canon 9 states that the laws issued by the Holy See are promulgated in the official organ of the Holy See, the *Acta Apostolicae Sedis,* and that the laws thus promulgated evince their force *(exserunt)* only upon the lapse of three months from the date appearing on the issue of the periodical which contains the newly formulated law, unless the nature of a particular law is such that its immediate enforcement is evident, or the law itself explicitly or specially provides for a longer or shorter period of suspension. The Holy See grants this period in order that the law may be sufficiently divulged; however, from the time of its promulgation the law effects an objective obligation in regard to the subjects.

2. Whenever laws are promulgated and the legislator does not grant a *vacatio,* it seems that the presumption that the law is known commences with the completed act of promulgation. However, a legislator will act prudently if he postpones the obligation attached to his laws until he is morally certain that they have become known to the community.[54] However, in the event that such a law is violated immediately after its promulgation, inculpable ignorance can quite readily be alleged, and at times also be accepted as an excuse.

It seems, therefore, that ignorance of law is not to be presumed after the effected promulgation whenever the legislator does not grant a *vacatio*. But when the lawmaker, in order that his legis-

---

c. 2, X, *de constitutionibus*, I, 2, n. 7; Pirhing, *Ius Canonicum Nova Methodo Explicatum*, lib. I, tit. I, sect. I, § 4, n. 30; Lohmuller, *The Promulgation of Law*, p. 12, footnote 22.

[54] Vermeersch-Creusen, *Epitome Iuris Canonici*, I, 65: ". . . legislator humanus obligationem suae legis prudenter differre solet donec lex ipsi communitati moraliter innotescat."

lation may be sufficiently divulged, expressly states that the law does not bind until a certain date, the presumption which in canon 16, § 2, takes for granted the possession of knowledge regarding the law, does not begin to operate until the conclusion of the period of suspension. After that time the law is presumed to be known, and consequently anyone who pleads ignorance of the law must prove his allegation.

Canon 16, § 2, admits exceptions to this presumption, for it states that ignorance is *generally* not presumed. These exceptions date back to Roman Law, which presumed or at least readily admitted ignorance of the law among certain classes of people.[55] These presumptions had their roots in natural equity, and were subsequently recognized and incorporated into the common doctrine of the pre-Code canonists, who likewise extended a presumption of ignorance of the law to women and rustics, to ignorant and illiterate people, to soldiers and to minors.[56]

That the traditional interpretation should be applied to this presumption is deduced from the following considerations. The Code in canon 1687, § 1, grants to minors and to persons enjoying the privileges of minors the extraordinary redress of *restitutio in integrum,* i.e., reinstatement in their previous condition, when they are gravely injured; this extraordinary relief may be granted by the judge *ex officio.*[57] Furthermore, the Code when treating of some of these classes of persons as subjects of penal laws[58] expressly warns the judge that he should look not only to the subject matter and the gravity of the law, but also the factors of age, knowledge, education, sex, state of life and mental condition as affecting the delinquents. In another canon[59] the law exempts

---

[55] D. (49, 16) (3, 2); (2, 1) (7, 4); (29, 5) (3, 22); (22, 6) 9; (4, 4) 1.

[56] Prosper Farinacius, *Variarum Questionum et Communium Opinionum Criminalium Liber Sextus, Fragmentorum Pars Secunda* (Romae, 1621), lib. VI, P. II, nn. 20-21; Dominicus Cardinalis Tuschus, *Practicae Conclusiones Iuris* (3. ed., 8 vols., Lugduni, 1634) s. v. *ignorantia,* concl. XI, nn. 11-12, and concl. XIII; Reiffenstuel, *Tractatus de Regulis Juris,* ad R.J. 13 in VI°, nn. 20-21.

[57] Canon 1688, § 2; Cicognani, *Canon Law,* p. 594.

[58] Canon 2218, § 1.

[59] Canon 2230.

minors who have not attained the age of puberty from incurring *latae sententiae* penalties, and canon 2204 states that, unless the contrary is apparent, minority diminishes the liability of an offender in a progressively greater degree as it approaches infancy.

The judicial practice and jurisprudence of the Sacred Roman Rota indicates that the pre-Code interpretations in regard to ignorance of the law are still to be accepted as valid norms. This tribunal has admitted ignorance of law among women.[60] In another case the Rota referred to those to whom the law is generally unknown. As an example of the latter the illiterate *(rustici)* and women were explicitly mentioned.[61]

Furthermore, among the approved post-Code authors who recognize these exceptions to the presumptions are found the names of Van Hove (1872-1947),[62] Maroto (1875-1937),[63] Michiels,[64] Ojetti (1862-1932),[65] Vermeersch (1858-1936)-Creusen,[66] Brys,[67] Berutti,[68] Beste,[69] and others.

To what laws may these exceptions be applied? According to the traditional doctrine these exceptions extend only to purely positive laws. The authors unanimously agree that all who have reached the use of reason know the natural law.[70]

---

[60] S.R.R., *Southwarcen.* (nullitatis matrimonii), die 29 iul. 1926, coram R.P.D. Henrico Inattrocolo, dec. XXXV, n. 8—*S.R.R. Dec.*, XVIII (1926), 286.

[61] S.R.R., *Restitutionis in integrum et diffamationis*, die 19 ian. 1923, coram R.P.D. Petro Rossetti, dec. II, n. 3—*S.R.R. Dec.*, XV, (1923), 12. Cf. Vermeersch-Creusen, *Epitome Iuris Canonici*, I, n. 284.

[62] *De Legibus Ecclesiasticis*, p. 245.

[63] *Institutiones Iuris Canonici*, I, 469.

[64] *Normae Generales*, I, 353-354.

[65] *Commentarium in Codicem Iuris Canonici*, I, 132.

[66] *Epitome Iuris Canonici*, I, n. 284.

[67] *Juris Canonici Compendium*, I, 127.

[68] *Institutiones Iuris Canonici*, I (Taurini-Romae: Marietti, 1936), n. 63.

[69] *Introductio in Codicem*, p. 76.

[70] Cf. Billuart, *Tractatus de Peccatis*, dissert. V, art: II—*Summa Sancti Thomae Hodiernis Academiarum Moribus Accommodata* (ed. nova, cura Lequette, 9 vols. in 8, Parisiis: Lecoffre (1878-1904); Ganzalez-Tellez, *Commentaria Perpetua in Singulos Textus Quinque Librorum Decretalium Gregorii IX*, ad c. 9, X, *de clerico excommuni-*

A final exception occurs in which canonists have recognized a presumption of ignorance in regard to the law, namely, when the law itself labors under some obscurity or ambiguity or is entangled in difficulties or complications.[71]

This traditional doctrine is still applicable, but within narrow limits, since the Code has clarified a great number of legal obscurities. The present law makes explicit provision for doubtful laws in canon 15, which states that all laws, including those invalidating and disqualifying laws, lose their binding force when a *dubium iuris* is present. In regard to the interpretations of ecclesiastical laws that are doubtful or obscure, canon 18 provides that recourse should be had to parallel passages in the Code if there are any, or to the purpose of the law and its circumstances, and the intention of the legislator.

Ignorance cannot be presumed on the part of one who is versed in the law, or on the part of one who holds an office, nor may he be presumed to be ignorant of those things which pertain to his office. In the first place, the knowledge of the affairs of one's office or position is presumably easy to obtain. If a man is not qualified for a certain post, e.g., of judge, confessor, administrator or pastor, he is bound to give it up when he realizes his limitations.

Canonists have long held the traditional view that ignorance with reference to the duties of one's state in life or of one's office is crass ignorance,[72] and moreover some moral theologians have

---

cato, vel interdicto ministrante, V, 27, n. 3; Reiffenstuel, *Jus Canonicum Universum*, ad Reg. Jur. 13 in VI°, n. 14; Mascardus, *De Probationibus*, Vol. II, concl. 640, nn. 4, 5; Menochius, *De Praesumptionibus*, lib. VI, praesumpt. XXIII, n. 23; Durandus, *Speculum Iuris*, lib. IV, partitio I, *de summa Trinitate*, n. 5.

[71] Maroto, *Institutiones Iuris Canonici*, I, n. 403, ad 3; *Reiffenstuel, Tractatus de Regulis Juris*, ad Reg. Jur. 13 in VI°, n. 22.

[72] Berutti, *Institutiones Iuris Canonici*, Vol. VI, *De Delictis et Poenis* (Taurini-Romae: Marietti, 1938), p. 27; Vermeersch-Creusen, *Epitome Iuris Canonici*, III, n. 249; Matthaeus Conte a Coronata, *Institutiones Iuris Canonici* (5 vols.; Vols. III-V, 1933-1936, Taurini: Marietti), IV, 33. Cf. also Passerinus, *Commentaria*, lib. I, tit. II, cap. II, q. I, art. 6, n. 145; Sylvester de Prierio, *Summa Summarum* (Venetiis, 1601), s. v. *ignorantia*.

classified the duties of one's state in life among the truths which must be known on their own account.[73]

In the external forum the presumption of knowledge of the law on the part of these persons is so strong that it can scarcely be rebutted. But even if the contrary is proved, the ignorance will most probably be considered as crass ignorance. However, in regard to individuals who have been well instructed in the law, experience shows that even those who were diligent in their studies and who once acquired the necessary knowledge may in later years forget what they once learned.

In conclusion it should be noted that this presumption is likewise found in most modern civil codes. The adoption of this presumption is attributed to social necessity and public policy. Occasionally the obligation to know the law is mentioned in relation to one's obligation to observe the law. Thus, "one who is bound to obey the law ought not to be allowed to say that he was ignorant of it . . . he cannot say that if the law had been as he supposed it to be, his act would have been lawful and he should not be punished."[74] And in another place, "every one competent to act for himself is presumed to know the law. No one is allowed to excuse himself by pleading ignorance . . . Courts are compelled to act upon this rule, as well in criminal as civil matters. It lies at the foundation of the administration of justice."[75] In practice, however, the civil authorities frequently mitigate these principles by treating such matters according to the rules of equity.[76]

The final matter to be considered in this article deals with the relationship between the presumption that the law is known, on

---

[73] Cf. Billuart, *Tractatus de Peccatis*, dissert. V, art. II; Suarez, *De Censuris*, disp. IV, sect. VIII, nn. 14-15—*Opera Omnia*, XXIII, p. 130.

[74] *State v. O'Neill*. 147 Iowa 513, 126 N.W. 454, 33 L.R.A. (N.S.) 788 (1910).

[75] *State v. Boyett*, 32 N.C. 336 (1849). Cf. Perkins, "Ignorance and Mistake in Criminal Law," *University of Pennsylvania Law Review*, LXXXVIII (1939-1940), 36-41; Keedy, "Ignorance and Mistake in Criminal Law," *Harvard Law Review*, XXII (1908-1909), 77-97; Swoboda, *Ignorance in Relation to the Imputability of Delicts*, p. 155, note 5.

[76] Cicognani, *Canon Law*, p. 595.

the one hand, and canons 12, 13 and 14, on the other. Canon 12 specifies those who are incapable of receiving ecclesiastical law; canon 13 treats of the subject of the law of the Church with respect to place; canon 14 considers strangers *(peregrini)*[77] and travelers *(vagi)*[78] as subjects of the law.

The three classes of persons specified in canon 12 as incapable of receiving *ecclesiastical* law are the following:

1. Those who are not baptized.
2. Baptized persons who do not have a sufficient use of reason.
3. Baptized persons who have the use of reason but who are under seven years of age, unless the law explicity rules otherwise.

Inasmuch as these persons are exempt by law itself, they are also exempt from the legal presumption in regard to knowledge of the law. Non-baptized persons are exempt because they have not received the sacrament of baptism through which one is constituted a member of the Church and a subject in relation to ecclesiastical authorities. Baptized persons who do not have a sufficient use of reason are not bound, as the natural law itself suggests, since they do not or cannot, in the case of the insane, understand the positive law. The exemption granted by law to the third group is based on the legal presumption enunciated in canon 88, § 3, which states that those who have not completed seven years of age are considered as not having attained the use of reason.[79]

It seems, however, that unbaptized persons who are not minors can be considered to have knowledge of certain ecclesiastical laws inasmuch as the existence of such laws is a *notorious fact.* Thus, for example, the ecclesiastical legislation in regard to divorce is a well known fact and is generally known to all.

Canon 13 states that *general* laws bind in every part of the world the persons for whom such laws were made. It also declares

---

[77] *Peregrini* are those who are actually outside the place of their domicile or quasi-domiciles—canon 91.

[78] *Vagi* are those who do not have a domicile or quasi-domicile anywhere—canon 91.

[79] Cf. Michiels, *Normae Generales*, I, 283-298; Cicognani, *Canon Law*, pp. 561-564; Vermeersch-Creusen, *Epitome Iuris Canonici*, I, n. 76.

that the laws which were given for a *particular* territory bind those for whom such laws were made and who have their domicile or quasi-domicile in that territory while they actually stay in that territory. From canon 16, § 2, therefore, it follows that all those to whom *general* laws apply or who are bound by *particular* legislation in virtue of canon 13 are indeed presumed to know such laws.

Finally, canon 14 treats of strangers *(peregrini)* and travelers *(vagi)* as subjects of law. The canon states:

1. Strangers are not bound by the *particular laws of their own territory* during their absence from this place, unless their transgression of the law does harm in their own territory, or unless the laws are personal.

2. Nor are strangers bound by the *particular laws of the place where they are actually staying* except by the particular laws which concern the public order or the solemnity of acts.

3. Strangers are bound by the *general* laws even though these laws are not in force in their own territory; but if the general law is not in force in the place in which they are strangers, although it is in force in their own territory, they are not bound by such general laws.

§ 2. Travelers *(vagi)* are bound by both the *general* and the *particular* laws in force in the place in which they are actually staying.

On the basis of canon 14, n. 1, it must be presumed that a stranger possesses knowledge concerning the laws of his own territory which are personal and also concerning those laws of his own territory the violation of which would cause harm to his own territory. This conclusion is strengthened further by the legislation of canon 13, § 1. However, it should be observed that if a person pleaded ignorance on the grounds that he was absent from his own territory ever since the time a particular law was promulgated, a judge could readily admit his plea, provided of course that he proved his allegation, unless another and a stronger presumption existed to the contrary.

On the basis of canon 16, § 2, with reference to number 3 of canon 14, a stranger is presumed to know those *general* laws which are effective in the place where he is a stranger, even though they are not enforced in the territory of his domicile or quasi-domicile. A stranger, however, on the basis of canon 14, n. 2, is *not* presumed to know the *particular* laws of the strange diocese, except those laws which consult the public order or which determine the solemnity of acts, e.g., the formalities to be observed in contracts. He is presumed to know the latter because such matters are of such gravity that their very nature certainly prompts any prudent man, even without previous knowledge, to suspect that any situation which involves the public order or any act which is normally observed with the performance of certain solemnities, is covered by a particular law of the place where he is sojourning.

Since canon 14, n. 2, mentions only these two instances in which strangers are bound by the particular laws of the place where they are staying, and since canon 16, § 2, makes no mention of other exceptions, it can be concluded that with reference to the diocese in which he is sojourning a stranger is presumed to know only those particular laws which consult the public order or which determine the solemnities of acts.

It is true that the existence of laws may be considered a notorious fact; however, according to the doctrine of the pre-Code canonists,[80] whose doctrine is very probably admissible at the present time also, ignorance of notorious facts was admitted in favor of those persons who did not belong to the community where the fact was published, or who were absent from a community when the notorious fact took place. Therefore, with the exception of those particular laws which regard the public order and the solemnities of acts, it does not seem in general that strangers should be presumed to know the law of the strange territory on the grounds that the existence of law is a notorious fact.

On the basis of canon 16, § 2, with reference to canon 14, n. 2, it seems logical to conclude that travelers *(vagi)* are presumed

---

[80] V. gr., Farinacius, *Variarum Questionum et Communium Opinionum Criminalium Liber Sextus, Fragmentorum Pars Secunda,* lib. VI, P. II, nn. 101, 102; Peckius, *Opera Omnia* (Antverpiae, 1666), *De Regulis Iuris,* R.J. 13, n. 3; Boich, *Commentaria,* ad c. 2, X, *de constitutionibus,* I, n. 2.

to know both the general and the particular legislation of the dioceses where they have their abode. Whether or not ignorance of the law is to be admitted in a particular instance is to be determined by the judge who examines the proofs which are offered by the traveler who pleads ignorance of the law.

ARTICLE 6. IGNORANCE OF THE PENALTY

In referring to this type of ignorance, canon 16, § 2, uses the phrase *ignorantia circa poenam.* Some authors have considered ignorance of the penalty as ignorance of law, namely, when one does not know in what the penalty consists, or as ignorance of the fact, namely, when one does not know that a penalty is attached to the law.[81] Several other authors prefer to place this type of ignorance in a category distinct from either ignorance of law or ignorance of fact.[82] However, ignorance of the penalty as mentioned in canon 16, § 2, is equivalent to ignorance of law, and consequently what has been said of the presumption regarding ignorance of law applies equally to ignorance of the penalty.[83]

Ignorance of the law has already been defined as the lack of knowledge concerning the law itself, its content, its meaning or its scope. By applying to this definition ignorance of the penalty, the different aspects of ignorance of the penalty become evident. Thus a person may be ignorant of the existence of a penal law; secondly, the prescription or prohibition may be known, but the person may not know the penal content of the law, namely, that a penalty is attached to the transgression of the law *(ignorantia poenalitatis);* thirdly, a person may be aware that a law is penal in character and yet may not know the specific nature or the meaning of the penalty contained in the law *(ignorantia naturae poenae).*

---

[81] Cicognani, *Canon Law,* p. 593; Toso, *Commentaria Minora,* I, 39.

[82] Michiels, *Normae Generales,* I, 349; Vermeersch, *Theologia Moralis,* I, 74; Noldin-Schmitt, *Summa Theologiae Moralis,* I, 57.

[83] Michiels, *Normae Generales,* I, 354; Ojetti, *Commentarium in Codicem Iuris Canonici,* I, 131; Regatillo, *Institutiones Iuris Canonici,* I, 66; Cocchi, *De Delictis et Poenis,* n. 4; Vermeersch-Creusen, *Epitome Iuris Canonici,* I, n. 88; Vermeersch, *Theologia Moralis,* I, 74.

The three subsequent sections consider ignorance of the penalty in reference to contumacy, to canon 2222, § 1, and to the penal precept.

1. Ignorance of the Penalty and Contumacy

There are certain crimes which postulate a determined subjective state, not because of the nature of the crimes themselves, but because of the nature of the penalty attached to them. Such is the case in respect to those penalties which are of the nature of censures, and with reference to which the subjective element is designated as contumacy.

Censures are medicinal penalties by which baptized persons who are contumacious and who have committed certain crimes are deprived of some spiritual or related temporal goods until these persons repent of their misdeeds and are absolved.[84] The legislator threatens the infliction of censures in order to prevent gravely serious external acts or in order to compel their subjects to perform some grave duties. When censures are incurred they are intended primarily to correct the delinquent, and only secondarily to repair the damage inflicted on the social order.

The three kinds of censures, namely, excommunication,[85] interdict[86] and suspension[87] can be so attached to a law or a precept that they are incurred *ipso facto* by the commission of the offense, or the law itself may command that they be inflicted by a judge or a superior. The former are called *latae sententiae* censures and the latter *ferendae sententiae.*[88] Furthermore, the law describes these penalties as *medicinal,* since they are directly intended to obtain the amendment of the delinquent; however, vindictive penalties are primarily instituted in order to repair the damage inflicted on the social or moral order through the violation of law.[89]

---

[84] Canon 2241.

[85] Cf. canons 2257-2267.

[86] Cf. canons 2268-2277.

[87] Cf. canons 2278-2285.

[88] Canon 2217, § 1, n. 2.

[89] Cf. canon 2216.

Excommunication is always a censure, while interdict and suspension can be either censures or vindictive penalties.[90]

In Roman Law contumacy was the term which designated the refusal of a person to appear in court after having been summoned by a judge.[91] This identical procedural law concept of contumacy was subsequently adopted by Canon Law.[92] Furthermore, it was applied to canonical *penal* law[93] and has come to signify the resolute disobedience and contempt of a delinquent who performs an action which he knows is forbidden and penalized in law.[94]

The nature of contumacy in respect to the medicinal penalties postulates that the delinquent be aware of the ecclesiastical law together with the penalty, namely, the censure. A person cannot be considered to have acted contumaciously, i.e., in contempt of law and his lawful superiors, unless he has knowledge of the legal prescription or prohibition and of the penalty attached to the violation of the law. Contumacy, therefore, always presupposes that a warning has been given.[95]

In the case of a *ferendae sententiae* censure the delinquent knows for certain the law and the exact penalty that will be inflicted in the event that the warning is disregarded. The law expressly demands that the judge or the superior administer an explicit

---

[90] Canon 2255.

[91] Cf. D. (37, 6), 110; (42, 1) 2; (42, 1) 53; (48, 19) 5.

[92] C, 1, C. IV, q.5; c. 6, C. XXIV, q. 3; cc. 2, 12, X, *de procuratoribus*, I, 38; c. 2, X, *de testibus et attestationibus*, II, 20; c. 1, *de appellationibus*, II, 15, in VI°.

[93] *Glossa Ordinaria* ad c. 23, C. XVII, q. 4, s. v. *praemissa*. Cf. Suarez, *De Censuris*, disp. IV, sect. VIII, n. 20—*Opera Omnia*, XXIII, p. 133; sect. IX, nn. 2, 14, 15, 19—*Opera Omnia*, XXIII, pp. 135 ff.; Pirhing, *Jus Canonicum*, lib. V, tit. XXXIX, sect. II, par. V, n. 45.

[94] Cf. Cappello, *Summa Iuris Canonici*, III, n. 230; Reiffenstuel, *Jus Canonicum Universum*, lib. V, tit. XXXIX, n. 14; Sole, *De Delictis et Poenis*, p. 82. In procedural law, contempt signifies the obstinate disobedience of a party to appear in court after he has been legitimately summoned. Cf. Cappello, *loc. cit.*; canons 1842; 1843, § 1; 1848; 1849.

[95] Cf. canon 2242, § 2; Ayrinhac-Lydon, *Penal Legislation in the New Code of Canon Law* (revised edition, New York: Benziger, 1936.), pp. 55-60; D'Annibale, *Summula Theologiae Moralis*, I, 322; Coronata, *Institutiones Iuris Canonici*, IV, 150-151.

warning before inflicting the penalty.[96] However, in the case of *latae sententiae* censures the warning is considered to have been given by the law itself. Canon 16, § 2, which establishes the presumption that the law and the penalty are known, reflects the principle on which the legislator relies when he institutes a penal law to which he attached a *latae sententiae* censure.[97].

2. *Ignorance of the Penalty and Canon 2222, § 1*

Penalties may be decreed by way of law or by way of precept;[98] secondly, they may be decreed as sanctions added to already existing laws;[99] finally, they may be imposed after the commission of a crime.[100]

When penal laws are properly promulgated, the subjects are presumed to know both the law and the penalty. If no penal sanction has been provided for in the law on the occasion of its promulgation, a penalty may be added subsequently if circumstances require it. Furthermore, canon 2222, § 1, states that even when a law does not indicate a penalty, a competent superior can nevertheless inflict a just penalty even without a previous warning if scandal has been given or the special gravity of the act deserves punishment.[101] Whenever the infliction of a penalty is not preceded with a canonical warning, it is evident that the penalty is not known. Consequently, in this instance the presumption enumciated in canon 16, § 2, does not apply. The legislator provided for this contingency in the latter canon when he expressed the presumption in the words, "ignorantia circa poenam *generatim* non praesumitur."

---

[96] Canons 2242, § 2; 2233, § 2.

[97] Cf. Coronata, *Institutiones Iuris Canonici*, IV, 150; Santi, *Praelectiones Juris Canonici*, lib. V, tit. XXXIX, n. 14; D'Annibale, *Summula Theologiae Moralis*, I, 322.

[98] Cf. canons 2195; 2220; 2310.

[99] Canon 2221.

[100] Canon 2222, § 1.

[101] Cf. Ayrinhac-Lydon, *Penal Legislation*, p. 33; Roberti, *De Delictis et Poenis* (Vol. I, pars 1, 1930; pars 2, 1938, Romae: Libraria Pontificii Instituti Utriusque Iuris), Vol. I, pars 1, pp. 70-76.

3. *Ignorance of the Penalty and the Penal Precept*

Canon 2195, § 2, indicates that penal sanctions may also be attached to precepts. A penal precept is a command which when given to an individual indicates to him accurately and in detail what he is to do or to avoid, and at the same time embodies the threat of a penalty in the event that the precept is transgressed.[102] The precise penalty which is threatened may be either a *latae* or a *ferendae sententiae* penalty, but before its observance can be prosecuted in a canonical trial the precept must be given in the form of a legal document or before two witnesses.[103]

Whenever a competent superior administers a penal precept to an individual, both the precept and the sanction are *de facto* known. Thus the legal presumption of canon 16, § 2, in regard to the penalty does not apply in this case, since presumptions of their very nature pertain to matters which are not certain. However, if it could be shown that the one who received the precept was insane on the occasion on which it was given, ignorance can readily be presumed.

ARTICLE 7. DOLUS AND THE PRESUMPTION OF KNOWLEDGE

Since laws are published by lawful authority in order that they will be observed, it is imperative that the subject inform himself on these laws, for otherwise he cannot fulfill his moral obligation of obedience to the commands and prohibitions of his lawful superiors. Three corollaries follow from this principle; namely, that the subject knows the law; secondly, that knowing the law he also knows the penalty attached to the penal law; and thirdly, that whenever he acts contrary to the law he does so willingly. These corollaries are expressed in the law as presumptions. Canon 16, § 2, embodies the first two, and the third appears in canon 2200, § 2, which states that when an external violation of the law occurs, *dolus* is presumed in the external forum until the contrary is proved.[104]

---

[102] Canon 2310.

[103] Canon 24.

[104] "Posita externa legis violatione, dolus in foro externo praesumitur, donec contrarium probetur."

Canon 16, § 2, and canon 2200, § 2, are parallel canons, but the latter is more particular in that it deals only with penal law, whereas the former deals with laws in general, with penal laws and with facts. Inasmuch as canon 16, § 2, mentions ignorance of the law and the penalty, it applies also to penal law. It must be observed moreover than canon 16, § 2, expressly admits the possibility of some exception to the ruling, for the word *generatim* is employed in the canon.[105] However, canon 2200, § 2, is worded absolutely, for it contains no such qualification. It should also be noted that the final presumption mentioned in canon 16, § 2, namely, that regarding non-notorious facts pertaining to others ignorance is presumed, constitutes an exception to the universal presumption of canon 2200, § 2.

However, the conflicts between the presumptions enunciated in these two canons are only apparent, and can be explained easily. Canon 16, § 2, presents a general rule, which has been placed in the First Book of the Code, which treats of the general norms of Canon Law. The presumption mentioned in canon 2200, § 2, is a particular presumption which modifies the general one;[106] consequently the legislator expressed it absolutely. Moreover, the *final* presumption enunciated in canon 16, § 2, is a particular presumption in relation to the rule expressed in canon 2200, § 2. In these instances the more specific presumptions prevail and have priority over the general rule. In these cases recourse must be made to the specific presumption rather than to the general presumption.[107]

It should be observed from the outset that the universal presumption of *dolus* is not equivalent to considering the accused to be guilty until he is proved innocent. On the contrary, the tribunal must first show that the accused actually committed the crime, and then the burden of proving that the act was not performed with *dolus* rests with the accused.[108] In assuming that the delin-

---

[105] Cf. Vermeersch-Creusen, *Epitome Iuris Canonici*, I, n. 88.

[106] Cf. Cappello, *Summa Iuris Canonici*, III, 449.

[107] Reg. 34, R. J., in VI°: "*Generi per speciem derogatur.*"

[108] Menochius, *De Praesumptionibus*, lib. V, praesumpt. III, nn. 45-48; Reiffenstuel, *Jus Canonicum Universum*, lib. I, tit. XXXVI, n. 5; Swoboda, *Ignorance in Relation to the Imputability of Delicts*, p. 180, note 77.

quent knows what he is doing and furthermore is aware of the moral, physical and juridical implications of his actions, the legislator is simply acting in accord with ordinary experience.

In the following paragraphs the notion of *dolus* will be briefly explained.[109] It will also be pointed out that there exists a type of *dolus* which is not identical with the type considered in canon 2200, § 2.

The word *dolus* appears in various canons throughout the Code.[110] Outside of the penal canons the word *dolus* is used in the Code in the sense of guile, deceit and deception;[111] in civil matters Roman Law employed this term in the same sense.[112]

In the penal law of the Code, canon 2200, § 1, furnishes the definition of *dolus,* namely, *"deliberata voluntas violandi legem."* Two elements enter into the constitution of *dolus:* first of all, a knowledge of the law or of one's legal obligation and an actual advertence to the act which is being performed contrary to the law, and, secondly, the deliberate intention of performing that act.[113] Knowledge of the penalty or of the penal character of the law is not required according to this legal definition.[114]

On the other hand, canon 2229, § 2, mentions a type of *dolus* which postulates *full knowledge* and *deliberation,* and which is distinct from the *dolus* described as *"deliberata voluntas violandi legem."* This type of *dolus* is postulated for certain crimes of such a serious nature that they are considered by the legislator as being

---

[109] Cf. Swoboda, *op. cit.*, pp. 89-102, for a complete and thorough analysis of *dolus.*

[110] Cf. canons 48, § 2; 52; 185; 542, n. 1; 572, § 1, n. 4; 1684, § 1; 1685; 1857, § 2, etc., which furnish examples wherein the word *dolus* differs in meaning from the same term as used in the Fifth Book of the Code.

[111] Cf. Cesare Badii, "Il dolo nel Codice de diritto canonico," *Il Diritto Ecclesiastico,* XL (1929), 305-326.

[112] D. (2, 14) (7, 9); (4, 3) (1, 2); the *Digest* also uses *dolus* in a good sense, e.g., referring to the cunning used to thwart a robber, as in D. (4, 3) (1, 3).

[113] Cf. Swoboda, *Ignorance in Relation to the Imputability of Delicts,* pp. 90-91.

[114] Cf. canon 2200, § 1; Cappello, *Summa Iuris Canonici,* III, 449.

committed only rarely, or the term is used in connection with laws which may readily be unknown.

It is clear that the Code distinguishes between two types of *dolus,* but it does not define the type mentioned in canon 2229, § 2. Commentators on the Code, however, have made use of a variety of expressions to designate this concept. Some of these are: *"special dolus,"*[115] *"perfect dolus,"*[116] and *"dolus plenissimus."*[117]

This type of *dolus* does not postulate a knowledge of the penalty or of the penal character of the law. Prior to the Code some authors[118] were of the opposite opinion. Cocchi, likewise, considered knowledge of the penalty as a constitutive element of this second type of *dolus,*[119] but this view leads to the unacceptable conclusion that when a delinquent is ignorant of the penalty he is exempt from incurring *ferendae sententiae* vindictive penalties. This is not the case, and furthermore it is contrary to the canonical principles regarding vindictive penalties.[120]

According to canon 2229, § 2, the laws which require full knowledge and deliberation contain the following expressions: *praesumpserit, ausus fuerit, scienter, studiose, temerarie, consulto egerit, aliave similia.* Swoboda enumerates and outlines the penal canons[121] which postulate perfect *dolus* as follows:[122]

> *Praesumpserit* is found in the following canons: 1625, § 2; 1755, § 3; 2321; 2338, § 1; 2346; 2347; 2365;

[115] Vermeersch-Creusen, *Epitome Iuris Canonici,* III, n. 219.

[116] Roberti, *De Delictis et Poenis,* Vol. I, pars 2, p. 276.

[117] Vermeersch-Creusen, *Epitome Iuris Canonici,* III, n. 248.

[118] Schmalzgrueber, *Ius Ecclesiasticum Universum,* lib. I, tit. II, n. 40; S. B. Smith, *Elements of Ecclesiastical Law,* Vol. III, *Ecclesiastical Punishments* (New York, 1888), pp. 32-33.

[119] *Commentarium in Codicem Iuris Canonici* (8 vols. in 5, 1920-1930, Liber V, *De Delictis et Poenis* (4. ed., Taurinorum Augustae: Marietti, 1938), n. 4 (hereafter cited *Commentarium,* VIII).

[120] Cf. Swoboda, *Ignorance in Relation to the Imputability of Delicts,* p. 175.

[121] It should be noted that the Code employs these expressions in canons whether enacting *latae* or *ferendae sententiae* penalties. Cf. Swoboda, *op. cit.,* pp. 174-175.

[122] *Op. cit.,* pp. 97-99.

2366; 2369, § 1; 2372; 2388; 2390, § 2; 2393; 2396; 2399; 2400; 2406; 2410; 2412, n. 1. *Scienter* is used in canons 2316; 2318, § 1; 2319, § 1, nn. 3, 4; 2326; 2338, §§ 2, 3; 2347, n. 3; 2360, § 1; 2362; 2368, § 2; 2371; 2390, § 2; 2391, §§ 1, 2, 3; 2395. *Ausus fuerit* occurs a few times, namely, in canons 2337, § 1; 2339; 2341; 2364; 2365; 2375.

The remaining three terms, *studiose, temerarie* and *consulto,* are not found in any of the penal canons of the Code. However, canon 2369, § 2, has a modified form of *temerarie,* namely, *temere.* This term presupposes perfect *dolus.* This is evident also from the fact the first paragraph deals with the direct violation of the seal of confession by the confessor. The second part of the canon concerns the violation of the sacramental seal by others than the confessor, and should consequently presuppose at least the same degree of subjective guilt.

While *studiose* does not occur expressly in any of the penal canons, it might be considered as implied in canons 2371 and 2392, which deal with simony. This crime according to the definition of simony in canon 727 presupposes a *studiosa voluntas.* Canon 2371 offers no difficulty, since it expressly uses the term *scienter,* and therefore demands perfect *dolus.* The omission of any qualifying term in canon 2392 might seem to indicate that perfect dolus is not stipulated as a condition for incurring the penalty of the law. However, in accord with pre-Code interpretation it can safely be held that also canon 2392 requires perfect *dolus.*

An accurate determination of similar expressions requiring perfect *dolus* offers some difficulty. There are four terms which canonists generally enumerate, namely, *pertinaciter, malitiose, fraude et dolo,* and *de industria.*

This enumeration seems to have begun with Chelodi and has been adopted by a number of the best canonists. Recently, however, some doubt has been cast upon two of these terms, namely, *de industria* and *fraude et dolo.* . . . However, on the basis of external authority it can scarcely be denied that the opinion of Chelodi and other is solidly probable.

How do these two types of *dolus* differ one from the other? The dolus mentioned in canon 2200, § 1, differs from the *dolus* mentioned in canon 2229, § 2, inasmuch as the former is presumed by law, once the objective commission of a crime has been proved. In the event that the delinquent pleads ignorance, he must prove it. On the other hand, the *dolus* which postulates *full* knowledge and deliberation does not seem to be presumed by the law, since knowledge and a direct will to perform the action prohibited by law are constitutive elements in the act, and consequently both the subjective state of the delinquent along with the facts of the case must be conclusively proved. Therefore, whenever a delinquent pleads ignorance the burden of the proof rests not with the individual but with the court.[123]

Inasmuch as the tribunal must prove that the delinquent acted with full knowledge, this case may be considered as an exception to the general presumption enunciated in canon 16, § 2, but an exception which the legislator envisioned when he expressed the latter presumption in the words *"ignorantia GENERATIM non praesumitur."*

ARTICLE 8. FACTA PROPRIA

Ignorance of fact simply means that physical or concrete events in general or the factual conditions for the application of the law are not known. The first type of ignorance of fact treated in this canon refers to *facta propria*. *Facta propria* can be defined as whatever is done through one's own personal agency and whatever an individual has personally sustained or experienced through his association with others.[124] The law presumes that a man knows the factual circumstances in which he acts. He is considered to be cognizant of his personal condition and affairs and to be aware of his own actions. Man is obliged to know such

[123] Swoboda, *op. cit.*, p. 177.

[124] Cocchi, *Commentarium*, I, n. 116: ". . . est factum quod quis posuit vel positive peractum a me elicitum, vel passive per actum a me passum."; Blat, *Normae Generales*, p. 94: ". . . factum proprium eo quod a seipso positum vel quod ipsius notabiliter interest." (The latter clause of this definition, however, is misleading, since such a fact could also be a *factum alienum*, and consequently this definition lacks precision.); Reiffenstuel, *Tractatus de Regulis* in VI°, R. J. 13: ". . . est qua facta nostra propria seu ea quae a nobis ipsis facta sunt."

facts because he is a responsible person. He is the master of his actions in virtue of his reason and his power of free choice.[125]

Knowledge, advertence, control, direction and freedom function in human actions. To the extent that these factors are absent, man's conduct fails to conform to his natural endowments. It is patent in everyday life that ignorance, error and inadvertence impair human activity; however, a legislator, in presuming that his subjects know their personal condition and the factual circumstances in which they act, bases his conjecture upon the nature of man as an agent endowed with self-consciousness, reason and free will.[126]

When the law explicitly states that ignorance is not presumed in regard to *facta propria,* it affirms the philosophical principle, namely, that whenever a man performs an action he is acting according to his nature as a man, that is, he knows what he is doing and he grasps the moral and physical implications of his actions.[127]

In regard to one's actions and personal condition, there should be certainty rather than ignorance; furthermore, the sources and authors[128] unanimously maintained this position before the Code, and the legislation of the Code in this regard is a complete restatement of the former law. This legal presumption provides the legal basis for the concept of human responsibility.

According to the common doctrine of canonists both before[129]

---

[125] Cf. *Summa Theologica,* Ia IIae, q. 1; Billuart, *Tractatus de Peccatis,* vol. II, dissert. V, art. II.

[126] Reiffenstuel, *Tractatus de Regulis Juris,* R. J. 47 in VI°: ". . . propria facta ignorare, nemo prudenter praesumitur."; Ojetti, *Commentarium in Codicem Iuris Canonici,* I, 132: ". . . acceditque obvia ratio, quia, sicut agens necessario habet conscientiam activitatis suae, si libere agit et humano modo, ita plerumque id meminit, nec praesumi potest ignorare."

[127] Cf. Michiels, *Normae Generales,* I, 354.

[128] Cf. D. (41, 10) 5; D. (16, 1) 7; Mascardus, *De Probationibus,* Vol. I, concl. 325, n. 25; Vol. I, concl. 554, n. 6; Vol. II, concl. 879, n. 40; Gonzalez-Tellez, *Commentaria Perpetua,* ad c. 9, X, *de clerico excommunicato, deposito, vel interdicto ministrante,* V, 27, n. 18.

[129] Menochius, *De Praesumptionibus,* lib. VI, praesumpt. XXIII, nn. 32, 38, 41, 47; Reiffenstuel, *Tractatus de Regulis Juris,* R. J. 13

and after[130] the Code, ignorance of one's personal affairs may be admitted in certain instances, for example, when the fact itself carries no particular significance or is of no serious importance to the individual.[131] In these and similar cases a lapse of memory and consequent ignorance is to be presumed. Furthermore, if a person becomes implicated in numerous and distracting affairs, it can be presumed by a judge or a superior that the person did not actually advert to the fact, especially when the matter is of little consequence. In other instances, when the fact itself is extremely complicated and detailed, intricate or involved, an ordinary person may be presumed by a *praesumptio hominis* not to understand.[132] However, such a presumption can be overthrown through the presentation of direct or indirect proof to the contrary.[133]

The presumption enunciated in canon 88, § 3, namely, that at the age of seven years a child has attained the use of reason, indicates at what time of a person's life the law considers him to be aware of his own actions. In the presumptions as stated in this canon, the legislator calls upon universal experience which shows that, in the vast majority of cases, the circumstance or fact of the age of seven years is accompanied with sufficient development and maturity to make a child responsible for its actions. In virtue of the same canon, a child under the age of seven years (he is called an *infans, puer,* or *parvulus*) is not responsible for his actions.[134] The fact which is presumed is the possession of the *use of reason;* the circumstance which points to the reasonableness of affirming that the use of reason exists is the definite circumstance of the completion of seven years of

---

in VI°, n. 11; Gonzalez-Tellez, *Commentaria Perpetua, loc. cit.*, and others.

[130] Maroto, *Institutiones Iuris Canonici*, I, n. 403, ad 2; Berutti, *Institutiones Iuris Canonici*, I, n. 63; Ojetti, *Commentarium in Codicem Iuris Canonici*, I, p. 132, n. 10; Regatillo, *Institutiones Iuris Canonici*, I, 66; Beste, *Introductio in Codicem*, p. 76.

[131] Cf. *opera citata.*

[132] Cf. *opera citata.*

[133] Cf. canon 1826.

[134] "Impubes, ante plenum septennium, dicitur infans seu puer vel parvulus et censetur non sui compos."—Canon 88, § 3.

age and the general experience that at this age a person has acquired the use of reason.[135]

This legal presumption can be vanquished directly or indirectly:[136] *directly,* through an examination of the fact which is presumed, namely, through a test of the *child's presumed use of reason* (as parents, pastor and confessor are supposed to do, on a certain basis, before admitting a child to First Holy Communion),[137] and *indirectly,* not through an examination of the fact itself which is presumed, but through a testing of the fact which serves as a basis for the presumption. The presumption that a child seven years of age has reached the use of reason would thus be *indirectly* vanquished through proof that the child is *not* seven years of age, for the age of the child is the fact or the circumstance which serves as the basis for the presumption that the child has reached the age of reason.

The legal presumption that ignorance is not presumed in regard to *facta propria* is related to another presumption which is derived from the natural law, but which is not explicitly expressed in the Code. The following presumption is more fundamental than the presumption enunciated in canon 16, § 2, and treated in this article, namely, that every man is presumed to be mentally normal by nature. Consequently, insanity is not presumed,[138] and whenever insanity is alleged, it must be proved directly or indirectly.[139]

---

[135] It should be observed in this connection that an *impubes,* i.e., a boy who has not completed his fourteenth year, or a girl who has not completed her twelfth year, is forbidden in view of a presumed immaturity of judgment to perform certain actions, e.g., to vote (canon 167, § 1, n. 2), to choose a church or a cemetery for burial (canon 1224, n. 1), to act as a witness (canon 1757, § 1), etc.

[136] Canon 1826.

[137] Canon 854, § 4.

[138] Menochius, *De Praesumptionibus,* lib. VI, praesumpt. XLV, n. 18: "Quae sane sententia probatur . . . et ratione, nempe, quod natura ipsa parit homines sanae mentis: et ideo qui asserit aliquem esse insanem repugnat ipsi naturae, atque ita ei adversatur praesumptio, quae a natura ipsa descendit. Et quae quidem praesumptio enum probationis onere gravat." Cf. Vermeersch-Creusen, *Epitome Iuris Canonici,* I, n. 88; Cocchi, *Commentarium,* VIII, 16.

[139] Menochius, *ibid.,* n. 22: "Cum ergo is qui asserit aliquem esse furiosum vel dementem, teneatur furorem et dementiam probare, at

When this fundamental presumption has become vanquished by proof to the contrary, the presumption that one is aware of *facta propria* is likewise defeated. Furthermore, whenever it has been proved that a person has been habitually insane, then all his past actions are considered to have been performed in ignorance.[140] Canon 2201, § 2, moreover, states that habitually insane persons are presumed to be incapable of committing an offense, even though they have occasional lucid moments or show signs of sanity in some of their reasoning or actions.[141]

ARTICLE 9. FACTA ALIENA

The second type of ignorance of fact treated in canon 16, § 2, is that which concerns happenings that occur in the lives of others *(facta aliena.)* The canon distinguishes between *facta aliena* which are *notoria* and those which are *non notoria,* and furthermore it is stated that ignorance is generally not presumed in regard to *facta aliena notoria,* whereas ignorance is presumed in regard to *facta aliena non notoria* until the contrary is proved.

The term *facta aliena* refers to all those matters which are not *facta propria,* i.e., it refers to things done by a third party.[142] The meaning of the word *notoria* in canon 16, § 2, is partially indicated in canon 2197, which defines an offense which is notorious by notoriety of law and an offense which is notorious by notoriety of fact. The latter canon states that an offense is notorious by notoriety of law after a sentence of a competent judge which has become irrevocable *(res iudicata),* or after a confession of a delinquent made in court in the manner prescribed in canon 1750,

---

poterit coniecturis seu signis, et praesumptionibus, quae eam inserunt, probari."

[140] Cf. Berutti, *Institutiones Iuris Canonici,* I, n. 63: ". . . de habitualiter amentibus contraria potius praesumptione censendum esse videtur quod generatim absque sufficienti deliberatione agant." The precise presumption of which Berutti speaks is a general presumption of man *(praesumptio hominis),* not a presumption of law, since it is not expressly stated in the law.

[141] Cf. Cocchi, *Commentarium,* VIII, n. 4; Coronata, *Institutiones Iuris Canonici,* IV, 31.

[142] Toso, *Commentaria Minora,* I, 40: ". . . id nempe quod ab alio actum est."

which defines a judicial confession, namely, an assertion of a fact made in writing or orally before the judge by one party against himself or in favor of the opponent, whether made of his own accord or in answer to a question of the judge.[143] An offense is notorious by notoriety of fact if it is publicly known and committed under such circumstances that it cannot be concealed through any subterfuge, or excused through any support deriving from the law.[144]

The word *notorium* should not be taken solely in the sense of canon 2197. The latter canon defines a notorious offense, while canon 16, § 2, treats of a notorious fact. The latter concept is far more extensive than the former. It is evident from the definitions expressed in canon 2197, that there are many facts which enter into the objective elements of delicts which cannot become notorious in the sense of a notorious offense.[145] Thus, for example, the fact that a particular building is a religious house with papal enclosure, or the fact that a person whom the offender strikes is a legate of the Roman Pontiff, are facts which do not become notorious in the sense of a crime. Nevertheless, the facts must be considered when a delinquent is accused of violating the law of enclosure or the *privilegium canonis.* If the word *notorium* in canon 16, § 2, is understood exclusively in the sense of *notorium* as this term occurs in canon 2197, it is being restricted to merely those facts of a criminal case which are by their very nature criminal in themselves. Such an interpretation of canon 16, § 2,

---

[143] Canon 2197, n. 2.

[144] Canon 2197, n. 3. Ojetti (*Commentarium in Codicem Iuris Canonici,* I, p. 132, ad 11) extends the application of notorious in canon 16, § 2, to notoriety of fact, but not to notoriety of law. Michiels, however (*Normae Generales,* I, p. 354, note 4), disagrees with Ojetti and remarks: ". . . hoc quod est notorium notorietate juris, regulariter in communitate vel regione, cujus interest, sine mora spargitur et notorium notorietate facti redditur." Cocchi (*Commentarium in Codicem Iuris Canonici,* I, 188), Toso (*Commentaria Minora,* I, 39), Blat (*Normae Generales,* n. 73) and others extend the word *notorium* in canon 16, § 2, both to law and fact. This latter view is that preferred by the present writer.

[145] Cf. canon 2197.

is too restricted and completely at variance with the purpose and tenor of the presumption.[146]

The precise significance of *notorium* cannot be derived from the definition of a *public* offense as defined in canon 2197, n. 1:

> An offense is public if it has already been divulged, or if it is committed under or attended with such circumstances that its divulgation may and must be considered as easily resulting.

The mere divulgation of a fact does not make it notorious, nor does the likelihood or the possibility that a fact will become public constitute an adequate basis for the presumption that such a fact is known. Actual publicity of the fact and a knowledge of the fact among the greater number of the group, community, etc., alone give rise to this presumption, so that it can very easily be known. The extent of the publicity depends on the circumstances. Thus a pertinent fact need only be divulged in a home to give rise to the presumption that it is known to an entire family. The same applies to a fact which has pertinence to a larger group, e.g., to an organization, a school, a parish, a city, and so forth.

The meaning of a notorious fact must be derived from the commonly accepted doctrine of the approved authors before the Code. Canon 6, n. 2, is the canon to be applied, and not merely canon 2197.[147] Canon 16, § 2, is a restatement of the former law, and for that reason must be interpreted according to the older law.

Facta aliena notoria refer to those matters and facts which are public or manifest, well known or important, when these facts are apparent to almost everyone, and when such facts can be known through the use of only ordinary diligence.[148] Three elements enter into the constitution of this concept.

---

[146] Cf. Swoboda, *Ignorance in Relation to the Imputability of Delicts*, p. 181.

[147] The precise meaning of a notorious delict was not established prior to the Code. Cf. Wernz, *Ius Decretalium*, VI, 21-22, note 35; Swoboda, *op. cit.*, p. 182, note 82.

[148] Reiffenstuel, *Tractatus de Regulis Juris*, R. J. 13 in VI°, n. 19: ". . . in casibus, et factis publicis ac notoriis, aut valde notabilibus

1. The fact itself must be publicly manifest or of an important or outstanding character.
2. It must be known to almost everyone in the group, the community, etc., as the occasion demands.
3. The knowledge of the fact must be easy of access, so that it can be learned through the use of ordinary diligence.

Swoboda states that since, as a general rule, ignorance of a *factum alienum* was presumed prior to the Code, the principle of canon 16, § 2, in which it is stated that ignorance is not presumed as regards *facta aliena notoria,* came into the Code as an exception.[149] The present writer finds it difficult to accept this statement of Swoboda, and he wishes to make the following observations concerning it.

It is indeed true that the traditional doctrine admitted the presumption of ignorance in respect to *facta aliena* but only in respect to *facta aliena non notoria.* This traditional doctrine, admitting a presumption of ignorance as regards *facta aliena non notoria,* was subsequently incorporated into canon 16, § 2: *ignorantia circa factum alienum non notorium praesumitur.* It does not seem, however, that the legislation of the Code regarding the presumption of knowledge in respect to *facta aliena notoria* should be considered, as Swoboda stated,[150] an exception to the pre-Code doctrine. One of the sources cited by Swoboda in support of his statement is Reiffenstuel (1642-1703).[151] In this context Reiffenstuel was speaking of *invincible* ignorance of a *factum alienum,* and it was to this type of ignorance that he applied the Regula Juris 13, "*ignorantia facti, non iuris, excusat.*" In this place Reiffenstuel stated: "*Unde etiam haec ignorantia facti alieni in judiciis semper praesumitur.*" This statement of Reiffenstuel per-

et ponderosis, quae fere cunctis patent, et a quovis modica dumtaxat adhibita diligentia sciri possunt." This is by far the best commentary on the significance of the term.

[149] *Op. cit.*, pp. 182-183: "According to the commonly accepted doctrine before the Code, the general rule was that ignorance of a *factum alienum* was presumed. The principle of canon 16, § 2, was stated as an exception to this general presumption . . ."

[150] Cf. *supra.*

[151] *Tractatus de Regulis Juris,* R. J. 13 in VI°, n. 10; Swoboda, *op. cit.*, p. 183, note 83.

haps furnished the basis for Swoboda's view that the general rule before the Code was that ignorance of *facta aliena* was presumed. However, it should be observed that, after stating that ignorance of a *factum alienum* is presumed, Reiffenstuel referred to the *Regula Juris* 47 in VI°, namely, *"praesumitur ignorantia, ubi scientia non praesumitur";* and in his commentary on the latter rule of law,[152] he noted that this *Regula Juris* 47 does not apply to notorious facts, or in other words that knowledge, not ignorance, is presumed as regards *facta aliena notoria.*[153] Reiffenstuel then referred to his commentary on *Regula Juris* 13, n. 19, in which he had stated that *Regula Juris* 13 *(ignorantia facti, non iuris, excusat)* does not apply to facts which are notorious and public, obviously for the reason that notorious and public facts are presumed to be known.

Indeed, the foundations for the presumption of knowledge as regards *facta aliena notoria* can be found in Roman Law,[154] and the same principle was repeated by the glossators.[155] Ioannes Andreae (1272-1348) in his commentary on the Rule of Law, *"praesumitur ignorantia, ubi scientia non probetur,"* expressly stated the presumption *"circa ea quae publice fiunt, praesumitur scientia,"*[156] which is fundamentally equivalent to the presumption in the Code, namely, *ignorantia circa factum alienum notorium non praesumitur.* Many other canonists also mention the presumption.[157]

From the foregoing considerations it is apparent that prior to the Code the distinction was made between *facta aliena notoria*

---

[152] *Op cit.*, R. J. 47 in VI°, n. 10.

[153] *Loc. cit.:* ". . . hic cum communi aliorum, quia in his non ignorantia, sed scientia praesumitur."

[154] "Latae culpae finis est non intelligere id quod omnes intelligunt."—(D. 50, 16) 223.

[155] V. gr., *Glossa Ordinaria* ad pr. D. XXXVIII, s. v. *cum itaque,* ad c. 14, D. XVI: ". . . nulli licet ignorare quae publice facta sunt."

[156] *Glossa* ad *Reg. Juris* 47 in VI°.

[157] Cf. Hostiensis, *Commentaria,* ad c. 13, X, *de electione et electi potestate,* I, 6 in Lib I, cap. 13, n. 13; Moroni, *Centum Responsa Centum Quaesitis,* Responsum LVI, n. 106; Reiffenstuel, *op. cit.* R. J. 47 in VI°, n. 10; Mascardus, *De Probationibus,* Vol. I, concl. 879, 35; concl. 637, n. 14.

and *facta aliena non notoria* and that the accepted doctrine was that knowledge was presumed as regards *facta aliena notoria* and ignorance was presumed as regards *facta aliena non notoria.* It can be concluded, therefore, that both of these presumptions were incorporated into the Code from the former legislation. However, the Code expressed these presumptions in more precise and restrictive language and thus brought to an end the confusion and ambiguity which the *Regulae Juris* tended to create during the pre-Code period.

Facta aliena non notoria pertain to those things which occur in the lives of others and which have not become publicly manifest so as to be known to all except to persons of leisure who are oversolicitous about the affairs of others.[158] Prior to the Code the Rule of Law, *"praesumitur ignorantia, ubi scientia non probatur,"* applied to these facts.[159] The Code clarified and incorporated this rule into the final legal presumption enunciated in canon 16, § 2, namely, *ignorantia circa factum non notorium praesumitur, donec contrarium probetur.* Ignorance is presumed in respect to *facta aliena non notoria,* because these facts are so numerous and diverse that they escape the notice even of observant and prudent persons.[160]

Authors have taken special cognizance of *facta aliena* which should be known in virtue of one's office, position or station in life.[161] It is vincible ignorance not to know those things which

---

[158] Berutti, *Institutiones Iuris Canonici,* I, 84: "Quae ad alios pertinent seu ab aliis peraguntur, si publice non sunt manifesta, ut plurimum non cognoscuntur nisi a viris otiosis et garrulis."

[159] Reg. 47, R. J., in VI°.

[160] Regatillo, *Institutiones Iuris Canonici,* I, 66; cf. also Gonzalez-Tellez, *Commentaria Perpetua,* ad c. 9, *de clerico excommunicato, deposito, vel interdicto ministrante,* V, 27, n. 18; Gulielmus Durandus, *Speculum Iuris,* lib I, partic. III, *de advocato,* n. 2; Michiels, *Normae Generales,* I, 355.

[161] Cf. *Glossa* ad c. 20, X, *de electione et electi potestate,* I, 6, s. v. *ignorantia;* Passerinus, *Commentaria,* lib. I, cap. II, q. I, art. 25; Moroni, *Centum Responsa Centum Quaesitis,* Responsum LVI, n. 106; Gonzalez-Tellez, *Commentaria Perpetua,* ad c. 9, X, *de clerico excommunicato, deposito, vel interdicto ministrante,* V, 27, nn. 3, 27; Reiffenstuel, *Tractatus de Regulis Juris,* R. J. 10 in VI°, n. 1; Regatillo, *Institutiones Iuris Canonici,* I, 66.

pertain to one's office or station.[162] For example, the members of an electoral group who place an unworthy candidate in office are presumed to be aware of his unfitness, since they are obliged to investigate his integrity and qualifications before casting their vote. The following rule applies in this instance: "*Non potest esse justa pastoris excusatio, si lupus oves comedat et pastor nesciat.*"[163]

When the facts which pertain to one's office or station in life are of a notorious character, they are presumed to be known because ignorance of notorious facts is generally not presumed. However, if these facts pertaining to one's office or station in life are *non-notorious,* a further distinction should be made, namely, into *non-notorious* facts which are *public* and *non-notorious* facts which are *occult.* It has already been shown that the word *notorium* in canon 16, § 2, does not apply to the meaning of *publicum* as used in canon 2197, n. 1; however, the words *publicum* and *occultum* in the sense of canon 2197 are acceptable subdivisions of the term *non notorium* as employed in canon 16, § 2.[164]

In view of this distinctionn between *non-notorious* facts which are *public* and *non-notorious* facts which are *occult,* it can be concluded that superiors and others are presumed to be aware of *public non-notorious* facts which pertain to their subjects. Moreover, it can likewise be deduced that everyone is presumed to know those *public non-notorious* facts which pertain to one's position or station. In the foregoing instances, if the public character of the non-notorious facts can be proved, the general

---

[162] Reiffenstuel, *Tractatus de Regulis Juris,* R. J. 13, in VI°, n. 6: ". . . in foro externo autem in quo quivis scire praesumitur id, quod illius status, conditio, aut officium requirit, omnis ille dicitur habere ignorantiam vincibilem, qui ea ignorat, quae scire ad statum et conditionem illius requiritur." Cf. also *ibid.,* n. 19.

[163] Reiffenstuel, *Tractatus de Regulis Juris,* R. J. 10 in VI°, n. 1: ". . . ignorantia illius, qui ex officio scientiam habere debet, et facile potest, pro crassa et culpabili reputetur. . . . Et ea, quae quis ex officio indagare tenetur, scire, et scire debere facileque posse, pro eodem habeantur."; Regatillo, *Institutiones Iuris Canonici,* I, 66.

[164] Regatillo (*Institutiones Iuris Canonici,* I, 66) seems to imply this distinction.

presumption contained in canon 16, § 2, regarding ignorance of *facta aliena non notoria* would thereby be overthrown.

The fact that superiors and other persons of a similar character are not presumed to know the *occult* facts regarding their subordinates has been the traditional doctrine and is also manifest in the final presumption mentioned in canon 16, § 2.[165] Never in the pre-Code history was knowledge of occult facts in the lives of others set up as a presumption of law. The contrary has always been the constant teaching of the canonists.[166]

---

[165] Reiffenstuel, *Tractatus de Regulis Juris*, R. J. 10 in VI°, n. 6: ". . . [Regula, i.e., *non potest esse justa pastoris excusatio, si lupus oves comedat et pastor nesciat*] fallit . . . in casu quo superior invincibiliter ignorat subditum in occulto male vivere et perire."

[166] Hostiensis, *Commentaria*, ad c. 1, X, *de postulatione praelatorum*, I, 5 in lib. I, tit. 4, c. 1, n. 21; Ioannes Andreae, *Glossa*, ad Regulam Juris XLVII in VI°; Mascardus, *De Probationibus*, Vol. II, concl. 879, n. 15.

CONCLUSIONS

1. The contents of both paragraphs of canon 16 have been incorporated into the Code from the former law.

2. The expression *ignorantia non praesumitur* as enunciated in canon 16, § 2, is equivalent to the expression *scientia praesumitur.*

3. The objective fact of promulgation and the force of law obliging those who are bound by it form the principal foundation for the legal presumption that ignorance of the law is generally not presumed.

4. The pre-Code exceptions to the presumption in regard to knowledge of the law still obtain in the present law, i.e., the exceptions regarding minors, women, soldiers, rustics and the like.

5. The presumption that the law and the penalty are known commences at the moment the promulgation has been effected, or at the termination of a *vacatio legis* if one was granted.

6. Those laws which contain expressions set forth in canon 2229, § 2, are exceptions to the presumption that ignorance of the law is not presumed. In these cases ignorance is presumed, since the burden of the proof rests with the court, and not with the delinquent.

7. The presumption as mentioned in canon 16, § 2, in regard to the law and the penalty is the principle on which the legislator relies when he institutes penal laws to which he attaches *latae sententiae* censures, for the latter penalties cannot be incurred unless the delinquent is previously warned.

8. The presumption as stated in canon 16, § 2, in regard to knowledge of the penalty does not apply with reference to canon 2222, § 1.

9. The presumption in regard to knowledge of the penalty does not apply to penal precepts given to individuals, since in this case the penalty is actually known.

10. The presumption that one is aware of his own actions and experiences *(facta propria)* has application when one has completed his seventh year.

11. Before a fact can be considered notorious it must be actually known to almost all the members of the group, society

or community to which it is pertinent, of interest, or of obligation, etc.

12. The final presumption enunciated in canon 16, §, namely, that ignorance of *facta aliena non notoria* is presumed, applies to two kinds of facts, both those which are occult and also those which are public, as long only as the latter have not in addition become notorious.

BIBLIOGRAPHY

Sources

Acta Apostolicae Sedis, Commentarium Officiale, Romae, 1909-

Bruns, C. G., *Fontes Iuris Romani Antiqui*, 7. ed., ab O. Gradenwitz, Tubingae, 1909.

Codicis Iuris Canonici Fontes cura Emi Petri Card. Gasparri editi., 9 vols., Romae (postea Civitate Vaticana): Typis Polyglottis Vaticanis, 1923-1939. Vols. VII-IX ed. cura et studio Emi Iustiniani Card. Serédi.

Corpus Iuris Canonici, ed. Lipsiensis 2., Aemilius L. Richter-Aemilius Friedberg, 2 vols., Lipsiae: Tauchnitz, 1879-1881. Ed. anastatice repetita, 1928.

Corpus Iuris Civilis, Vol. I, *Institutiones*—recognovit P. Krueger; Vol. II, *Codex Iustinianus*—recognovit et retractavit P. Krueger; Vol. III, *Novellae Constitutiones*—R. Schoell; opus Schoellii morte interceptum absolvit G. Kroll, Berolini: apud Weidmannos, 1928-1929.

——, *Digesta Iustiniani Augusti*—recognoverunt et ediderunt P. Bonfante, C. Fadda, C. Ferrini, S. Roccobono, V. Scialoia, Mediolani: Società Editrice Libraria, 1931.

Decretum Gratiani emendatum et notationibus illustratum una cum glossis, Romae, 1582.

Decretales D. Gregorii Papae IX, una cum glossis restitutae, Romae, 1582.

Denzinger, H.-Bannwart, C.-Umberg, J. B., *Enchiridion Symbolorum, Definitionum et Declarationum de Rebus Fidei et Morum*, 22-23. ed., Friburgi-Brisgoviae: Herder, 1937.

Girard, Paul, *Textes de Droit Romain*, 5. ed., Paris: Rousseau, 1923.

Hardouin, Jean, *Acta Conciliorum et Epistolae Decretales ac Constitutiones Summorum Pontificum*, 12 vols., Parisiis, 1714-1725.

Jaffé, Philippus, *Regesta Pontificum Romanorum ab condita Ecclesia ad annum post Christum natum MCXCVIII*, 2. ed. cura G. Wattenbach, S. Loewenfeld, F. Kaltenbrunner, P. Ewald, 2 vols. in 1, Lipsiae: Veit et Comp., 1885-1888.

Liber Sextus Decretalium, una cum Clementinis et Extravagantibus earumque glossis restitutis, Romae, 1582.

Mansi, Joannes, *Sacrorum Conciliorum Nova et Amplissima Collectio*, 53 vols. in 60, Parisiis, 1901-1927.

Potthast, Augustus, *Regesta Pontificum Romanorum inde ab anno Post Christum Natum MCXCVIII ad annum MCCCIV*, 2 vols., Berlini, 1874-1875.

S. Romanae Rotae Decisiones seu Sententiae (ab anno 1909), Romae, 1912-

Authors

Alexander Halensis, *Summa Theologica*, 3 vols., ed. PP. Collegii S. Bonaventurae, ad Claras Aquas: Typographia Collegii S. Bonaventurae, 1924-1930.

Alphonsus Liguori, St., *Theologia Moralis*, ed. L. Gaudé, 4 vols., Romae, 1905-1912.

Alterius, Marius, *De Censuris Ecclesiasticis*, 2 vols., Romae, 1618.

Ayrinhac, H. A., and Lydon, P. J., *Marriage Legislation in the New Code of Canon Law, New York:* Benziger Bros., Inc., 1932.

——, *Penal Legislation in the New Code of Canon Law*, revised edition, New York: Benziger, 1936.

Ballerini, Antonius, et Palmieri, Dominicus, *Opus Theologicum Morale*, 7 vols., Prati, 1889-1893.

Barbosa, Augustinus, *Collectanea Doctorum tam Veterum quam Recentiorum in Jus Pontificium Universum*, 5 vols. in 3, Lugduni, 1637.

——, *Praxis Exigendi Pensiones cui accesserunt Vota Plurima Decisiva et Consultiva Canonica*, Lugduni, 1663.

——, *Pastoralis Solicitudinis sive de Officio et Potestate Episcopi*, 3 vols. in 1, Lugduni, 1678.

Bargilliat, Michael, *Praelectiones Juris Canonici*, 2 vols., 37 ed., Parisiis: Apud Baston, Berche et Pagis, 1923.

Berutti, Christophorus, *Institutiones Iuris Canonici*, Vol. I, *Normae Generales*, 1936; Vol. VI, *De Delictis et Poenis*, 1938, Taurini-Romae: Marietti.

Beste, Udalricus, *Introductio in Codicem*, 3. ed., Collegeville, Minn.: St. John's Abbey Press, 1946.

Billuart, F.C.R., *Summa Sancti Thomae Hodiernis Academiarum Moribus Accommodata*, ed. nova, cura Lequette, 9 vols. in 8, Parisiis: Lecoffre, 1878-1904.

Binding, K., *Normen und ihre Uebertretung*, Leipzig, 1872-1888.

Blat, Albertus, *Commentarium Textus Codicis Iuris Canonici*, 5 vols. in 6, Romae, 1921-1927; Liber I, *Normae Generales*, 1921; Liber III, Pars I, *De Sacramentis*, 2 ed., 1924; Liber V, *De Delictis et Poenis*, 1924, Romae: Collegio "Angelico".

Boich, Henricus, *In Quinque Decretalium Libros Commentaria*, Venetiis, 1576.

Bonaventura, St., *Commentaria in IV Libros Sententiarum*, ed. minor, ad Claras Aquas: Typographia Collegii S. Bonaventurae, 1934-1938.

Bouquillon, Thomas, *Theologia Moralis Fundamentalis*, 2. ed., Brugis, 1890.

Buckland, W. W., *A Textbook of Roman Law*, Cambridge, 1921.

Brys, Josephus, *Juris Canonici Compendium*, Brugis: Desclée De Brouwer et Sii, 1947.

Cance, Adrien, *Le Code de Droit Canonique, Commentaire succinct et pratique*, 5. ed., 3 vols., Paris: Lecoffre, 1930.

Capello, Felix, *De Censuris iuxta Codicem Iuris Canonici*, 3. ed., Taurinorum Augustae: Marietti, 1933.

——, *Summa Iuris Canonici*, 3 vols.; Vol. I, 4. ed., 1945; Vol. III, 2. ed., 1940, Romae: Apud Aedes Universitatis Gregorianae.

——, *Tractatus Canonici-Moralis de Sacramentis*, 5 vols.; Vol. V, *De Matrimonio*, 5. ed.; Vol. IV, *De Ordine*, 2. ed., Augustae Taurinorum, Romae: Marietti, 1947.

Cerato, Prosdocimus, *Censurae Vigentes Ipso Facto a Codice Iuris Canonici Excerptae*, 2. ed., Patavii: Typis Seminarii, 1921.

Chelodi, Ioannes, *Ius Canonicum de Matrimonio*, 5. ed., a Pio Cipratti, Vicenza: Società Anonima Tipografica Editrice, 1947.

——, *Ius Matrimoniale iuxta Codicem Iuris Canonici*, 3. ed., Tridenti: Libr. Edit. Tridentum, 1921.

——, *Ius Poenale et Ordo Procedendi in Iudiciis Criminalibus*, 4. ed., a Vigilia Dalpiaz, Tridenti: Ardesi, 1935.

Cicognani, Amletus, *Canon Law*, authorized English version, by J. O'Hara and F. Brennan, 2nd revised edition, Philadelphia: Dolphin Press, 1935.

Cipollini, Albertus, *De Censuris Latae Sententiae iuxta Codicem Iuris Canonici*, Taurini: Marietti, 1925.

Cocchi, Guidus, *Commentarium in Codicem Iuris Canonici*, 8 vols. in 5, 1920-1930; Liber I, *Normae Generales*, 3. ed., 1925; Liber IV, *De Processibus*, 3. ed., 1940; Liber V, *De Delictis et Poenis*, 4. ed., 1938, Taurinorum Augustae: Marietti.

Coffey, Peter, *The Science of Logic*, 2nd impression, 2 vols., London-New York: Longmans, Green& Co., 1918.

Coronata, Matthaeus, Conte a, *Institutiones Iuris Canonici*, 5 vols.; Vols. I-II, 2. ed., 1939; Vols. III-V, 1933-1936, Taurini: Marietti.

Covarrubias y Leyva, Didacus, *Opera Omnia*, 2 vols., Coloniae Allobrogum, 1679.

Creighton, J. E., and Smart, H. R., *Introductory Logic*, 5. ed., New York: Macmillan Co., 1932.

D'Angelo, S., *Ius Digestorum*, 2 vols., Romae, 1927-1928.

D'Annibale, Josephus, *Summula Theologiae Moralis*, 5. ed., 3 vols., Romae, 1908.

De Becker, Julius, *De Sponsalibus et Matrimonio Praelectiones Canonicae*, Bruxellis, 1896.

Durandus, Gulielmus, *Speculum Iuris*, 4 vols. in 3, Venetiis, 1577.

Fagnanus, Prosper, *Commentaria in Quinque Libros Decretalium*, 4 vols., Romae, 1661.

Falchi, Giuseppino, *Diritto Penale Romano, Dottrine Generali*, Treviso: Vianello, 1930.

Farinacius, Prosper, *Variarum Quaestionum et Communium Opinionum Criminalium Liber Sextus, Fragmentorum Pars Secunda*, Romae, 1621.

Ferraris, Lucius, *Prompta Bibliotheca Canonica, Iuridica, Moralis, Theologica, nec non Ascetica, Polemica, Rubricistica, Historica*, 9 vols., Romae, 1885-1899.

Ferrini, Contardo, *Diritto Penale Romano, Teorie Generali*, Milano, 1899.

——, *Manuele di Pandette*, 3. ed., Milano, 1921.

Gabriel a S. Vincentio, *De Remediis Ignorantiae*, Romae, 1671.

Gaius, *Institutiones*, 6. ed., E. Seckel-B. Kuebler, Lipsiae: Teubner, 1928.

Gasparri, P,. *Tractatus de Sacra Ordinatione*, 2 vols, Parisiis, 1893.

Girard, P., *Manuel Elémentaire de Droit Romain*, 7. ed., Paris, 1924.

Gonzalez-Tellez, Emmanuel, *Commentaria Perpetua in Singulos Textus Quinque Librorum Decretalium Gregorii IX*, 5 vols. in 4, Lugduni, 1715.

Gougnard, A., *Tractatus de Matrimonio*, 7. ed., Mechliniae, 1931.

Heiner, Franz, *Katholisches Kirchenrecht*, 5. ed., 2 vols., Paderborn, 1909.

Hickey, J. S., *Summula Philosophiae Scholasticae*, 3 vols.; Vol. I, 4. ed., Dublin, 1915.

Hinschius, Paul, *Das Kirchenrecht der Katholiken und Protestanten in Deutschland*, 6 vols., Berlin, 1869-1897.

Hollweck, Joseph, *Die kirchlichen Strafgesetze*, Mainz, 1899.

Hostiensis, Cardinalis (Henricus de Segusio), *Commentaria in Quinque Decretalium Libros*, 5 vols. in 3, Venetiis, 1581.

Ioannes Andrea, *In Sex Decretalium Libros Novella Commentaria*, 6 vols. in 5, Venetiis, 1581.

Jolowicz, H. F., *Historical Introduction to the Study of Roman Law*, Cambridge: University Press, 1932.

Kantorowicz, Hermann, with the collaboration of W. W. Buckland, *Studies in the Glossators of Roman Law*, Cambridge: University Press, 1938.

Kelly, James, *The Jurisdiction of the Simple Confessor*, New York: Benziger Bros., 1929.

Kuttner, Stephan, *Kanonistische Schuldlehre von Gratian bis auf die Dekretalen Gregors IX*, Studi e Testi, n. 64, Città del Vaticano: Biblioteca Apostolica Vaticana, 1935.

Leage, R. W., *Roman Private Law*, 2. ed., by C. H. Ziegler, London: Macmillan & Co., 1946.

Lega, M., *De Delictis et Poenis*, 2. ed., Romae, 1910.

Lehmkuhl, Augustinus, *Theologia Moralis*, 5. ed., 2 vols., Friburgi Brisgoviae, 1888.

Liddell, H. G.-Scott, R., *Greek-Latin Lexicon*, 8. ed., New York: American Book Co., 1897.

Lohmuller, M. J., *The Promulgation of Law*, The Catholic University of America Canon Law Studies, n. 241, Washington, D. C.: The Catholic University of America Press, 1947.

Maroto, Philippus, *Institutiones Iuris Canonici*, 2 vols., 1919; Vol. I, 3. ed., 1921, Romae: Apud Commentarium pro Religiosis.

Mascardus, Josephus, *De Probationibus*, 3 vols., Venetiis, 1593-1595.

Menochius, Jacobus, *De Praesumptionibus, Coniecturis, Signis, et Indiciis Commentaria* 2 vols., Coloniae Allobrogum, 1686.

Michiels, Gommarus, *Normae Generales Iuris Canonici*, 2 vols., Lublin: Universitas Catholica, 1929.

——, *De Delictis et Poenis*, Vol. I, *De Delictis*, Lublin: Universitas Catholica, 1934.

Migne, Jacques P., *Patrologiae Cursus Completus, Series Graeca*, 162 vols., Parisiis, 1857-1866.

——, *Patrologiae Cursus Completus, Series Latina*, 221 vols., Parisiis, 1844-1864.

Mommsen, Theodore, *Le Droit Pénal Romain*, trans. by J. Duquesne, 3 vols., Paris, 1907.

Moroni, Illuminatus, *Centum Responsa Centum Quaesitis*, Mediolani, 1682.

Mueller, O., *Sexti Pompeii Festi de Verborum Significatione quae supersunt*, Lipsiae, 1839.

Müller, Michael, *Ethik und Recht in der Lehre von der Verantwortlichkeit*, Regensburg: Josef Habbel, 1932.

Navarrus (Martinus de Azpilcueta), *Consiliorum sive Responsorum Libri Quinque*, Romae, 1602.

Newman, John Henry Card., *Grammar of Assent*, Longmans, Green & Co., 1903.

Noldin, H., et Schmitt, A., *Summa Theologiae Moralis*, 3 vols.; Vol. I, 26. ed., 1939; Vols. II-III, 25. ed., 1938, Oeniponte: Rauch.

Ojetti, Benedictus, *Commentarium in Codicem Iuris Canonici*, 4 vols., Romae: Universitas Gregoriana, 1927-1931.

Panormitanus, Abbas (Nicholaus de Tudeschis), *Commentaria in Quinque Libros Decretalium*, 5 vols. in 7, Venetiis, 1588.

Passerinus, Petrus, *Commentaria in Sextum Librum Decretalium*, 1698.

Paucapalea, *Summa*, ed. J. F. von Schulte, Giessen, 1890.

Peckius, Petrus, *Opera Omnia*, Antverpiae, 1666.

Pellé, M. L'Abbé, P., *Le Droit Pénal de L'Église*, Paris: Lethielleux, 1939.

Petrus Lombardus, *Libri Quatuor Sententiarum*, 2. ed., 2 vols., PP. Collegii S. Bonaventurae, ad Claras Aquas: Typographia Collegii S. Bonaventurae, 1916.

Pichler, Vitus, *Candidatus Jurisprudentiae Sacrae*, 3. ed., 5 vols., 1723-1728; Vol. I, 4. ed., 1733, Augustoduni.

——, *Jus Canonicum secundum quinque Decretalium Titulos Gregorii Papae IX Explicatum*, 2 vols. in 2, Ravennae, 1741.

Pighi, J. B., *Censurae Sententiae Latae et Irregularitates*, 7. ed., Veronae: Sorores Cinquetti Filiae Felicis, 1922.

Pirhing, Ernricus, *Jus Canonicum Nova Methodo Explicatum*, 5 vols. in 4, Dilingae, 1674-1678.

Prümmer, Dominicus, *Manuale Theologiae Moralis*, 8. ed., cura Engelberti Münch, 3 vols., Friburgi Brisgoviae: Herder, 1935-1936.

Regatillo, Eduardus, *Institutiones Iuris Canonici*, 2 vols., Santander: Sal Terrae; Vol. I, 2. ed., 1946; Vol. II, 1942.

Reiffenstuel, Anacletus, *Jus Canonicum Universum*, 7 vols., Parisiis, 1864-1870.

Roberti, Franciscus, *De Delictis et Poenis*, Vol. I, pars 1, 1930; pars 2, 1938, Romae: Libraria Pontificii Instituti Utriusque Iuris.

Rufinus, *Summa Decretorum*, ed. H. Singer, Paderborn, 1902.

Salmanticenses, *Cursus Theologiae Moralis*, 6 vols. in 4, Venetiis, 1714-1728.

Salucci, Raffaele, *Il Diritto Penale secondo il Codice di Diritto Canonico*, 2 vols., Subiaco: Tipografia dei Monasteri, 1926-1930.

Sanchez, Thomas, *De Sancto Matrimonii Sacramento*, 3 vols. in 2, Antverpiae, 1607.

Santi, Franciscus, *Praelectiones Juris Canonici*, 5 vols. in 2, Ratisbonae, 1886.

Savigny, F. K., *System des heutigen römischen Rechts*, 8 vols., Berlin, 1840-1849.

Schmalzgrueber, Franciscus, *Jus Ecclesiasticum Universum*, 5 vols. in 12, Romae, 1843-1845.

Schmitz, H. J. *Die Bussbücher und die Bussdisciplin der Kirche*, 2 vols., Mainz, 1883-1898.

Schroeder, H. J., *Disciplinary Decrees of the General Councils*, St. Louis: Herder, 1937.

Smith, S. B., *Elements of Ecclesiastical Law;* Vol. III, *Ecclesiastical Punishments*, New York, 1888.

Sole, Jacobus, *De Delictis et Poenis*, Romae: Pustet, 1920.

Stephanus, Tornacensis, *Summa*, ed. J. F. von Schulte, Giessen, 1891.

Suarez, Franciscus, *Opera Omnia*, 28 vols., Parisiis, 1856-1861.

Swoboda, Innocent Robert, *Ignorance in Relation to the Imputability of Delicts*, The Catholic University of America Canon Law Studies, n. 143, Washington, D. C.: The Catholic University of America Press, 1941.

Sylvester de Prierio (Mozolinus Sabaudus), *Summa Summarum*, Venetiis, 1601.

Thesaurus, Carolus, et Giraldi, Ubaldus, *De Poenis Ecclesiasticis*, nova editio, Romae, 1831.

Thomas Aquinas, St., *Summa Theologica*, diligenter emendata et Nicolae, Sylvii, Billuart et C. J. Drioux notis ornata, 6. ed., 8 vols., Barri-Ducis, 1870.

Torre, Joannes, *De Pactis Futurae Successionis Tractatus Tripartitus*, 3 vols. in 1, Venetiis, 1694.

Toso, Albertus, *Ad Codicem Iuris Canonici Commentaria Minora*, Vol. I, 2. ed., Taurini, Romae: Marietti, 1921.

Tuschus, Dominicus Cardinalis, *Practicae Conclusiones Iuris*, 3. ed., 8 vols., Lugduni, 1634.

Van Gestel, A., *De Justitia et Lege Civili*, Groningae, 1896.

Van Hove, A., *Commentarium Lovaniense in Codicem Iuris Canonici;* Vol. I, Tom. II, *De Legibus Ecclesiasticis*, Mechliniae: H. Dessain, 1930.

Vermeersch, A., Creusen, J., *Epitome Iuris Canonici*, Vol. I, 6. ed., 1937; Vols. II-III, 5. ed., 1934-1936, Mechliniae: H. Dessain.

Vermeersch, Arturus, *Theologiae Moralis Principia, Responsa, Concilia*, 3. ed., 4 vols., Romae: Universitas Gregoriana, 1933-1937.

——, *Quaestiones de Justitia*, Brugis, 1901.

Wernz, Franciscus, *Ius Decretalium*, 2. ed., 6 vols., Romae et Prati, 1906-1913.

Wernz, Franciscus, et Vital, Petrus, *Ius Canonicum*, 7 vols. in 8, Romae: Universitas Gregoriana, 1923-1938; Vol. I, 1938; Vol. II, 1923; Vol. V, 1925; Vol. VII, 1937.

Articles

Amann, "Penitence," *Dictionnaire de Théologie Catholique*, XII (1936), 789.

Badii, Cesare, "Il dolo nel Codice di diritto canonico," *Il Diritto Ecclesiastico*, XL (1929), 305-326.

Galtier, Fr., "De Ignorantia et errore in censurarum specialissimo modo reservatarum absolutione," *Periodica*, XVII (1928), 55*-68*.

Keedy, Edwin, "Ignorance and Mistake in the Criminal Law," *Harvard Law Review*, XXII (1908), 75-96.

Lottin, D. O., "Le problème de l'*ignorantia iuris* de Gratien à St. Thomas d' Aquin," *Recherches de Théologie ancienne et médiévale*, V (1933), 345-368.

Montes, J., "La ignorancia en el derecho penal," *Ciudad de Dios*, CXLIX (1927), 43-60; 213-226.

O'Neill, "Ignorance of Ecclesiastical Laws and Punishments," *IER*, 5. series, XXIX (1927), 292-293.

Perkins, Rollin M., "Ignorance and Mistake in Criminal Law," *University of Pennsylvania Law Review*, LXXXVIII (1939-1940), 35-70.

Pernice, Alfred, "Der verbrecherische Vorsatz im griechisch-römischen Rechte," *Zeitschrift der Savigny-Stiftung*, XVII (1896), 205-251.

Toso, A., "De Errore Communi," *Jus Pontificium*, III (1923), 150-164.

PERIODICALS

Ciudad de Dios, La (formerly, *Revista Agustiniana* [13 vols., 1881-1887], Valladolid, 1881-1889; Madrid, 1890-

Diritto Ecclesiastico, Il, Romae, 1890-

Harvard Law Review, Cambridge, Mass., 1887-

Jus Pontificium, Romae, 1921-1940.

Periodica de Re Canonica et Morali utilia praesertim Religiosis et Missionariis, Brugis, 1905-1927.

Recherches de Théologie Ancienne et Médiévale, Louvain, 1929-

Zeitschrift der Savigny-Stiftung für Rechtgeschichte, Weimar, 1880.

ABBREVIATIONS

AAS—*Acta Apostolicae Sedis.*
C.—*Codex (Iustinianus).*
CSEL—*Corpus Scriptorum Ecclesiasticorum Latinorum.*
D.—*Digesta.*
Fontes—*Codicis Iuris Canonici Fontes* cura . . . Gasparri editi.
Hardouin—*Acta Conciliorum, etc.*
IER—*Irish Ecclesiastical Record.*
Jaffé—*Regesta Pontificum Romanorum ad annum 1198.*
Mansi—*Sacrorum Conciliorum Nova et Amplissima Collectio.*
MPG—Migne, *Patrologia Graeca.*
MPL.—Migne, *Patrologia Latina.*
Periodica—*Periodica de Re Canonica et Morali.*
Potthast—*Regesta Pontificum Romanorum* anno 1198 ad annum 1304.
S.R.R. Dec.—*S.R. Rotae Decisiones seu Sententiae* (ab. a. 1909).

ALPHABETICAL INDEX

BIOGRAPHICAL NOTE

Michael J. Regan was born on November 22, 1921 in Philadelphia, Pennsylvania. He received his elementary education at St. Columba's and Corpus Christi Parochial Schools in Philadelphia. He attended Roman Catholic High School in that city. His philosophical and theological studies were made at St. Charles Borromeo Seminary in Overbrook, Philadelphia, Pennsylvania. He was ordained to the priesthood on May 30, 1946. In September, 1946, he entered the School of Canon Law at the Catholic University of America, from which he received the degree of Baccalaureate in Canon Law in June, 1947, and the degree of Licentiate in Canon Law in June, 1948. After his completion of the Canon Law course in June, 1949, he returned to Philadelphia and was assigned to teach at Southeast Catholic High School, Philadelphia, where he remained until March, 1950, when he was sent on a temporary assignment to the former Diocese of Savannah-Atlanta in Georgia. There he was connected with the Diocesan Tribunal in the capacity of notary. In November, 1956, upon the division of the Diocese of Savannah-Atlanta into two separate jurisdictions, he was transferred to Atlanta and there appointed Officialis of the Diocese of Atlanta. In July, 1958, he was excardinated from the Archdiocese of Philadelphia and incardinated into the Diocese of Atlanta.

CANON LAW STUDIES*

286. O'BRIEN, REV. KENNETH R., A.B., J.C.D., The Nature of Support of Diocesan Priests in the United States, XVI-162 pp., 1949.
287. METZ, REV. JOHN E., S.T.L., J.C.D., The Recording Judge in the Ecclesiastical Collegiate Tribunal, X-130 pp., 1949.
288. REINHARDT, REV. MARION J., S.T.L., J.C.D., The Rogatory Commission, XIII-182 pp., 1949.
289. ORTEGA UHIUK, REV. JUAN, S.J., J.C.D., De Delicto Sollicitationis.
290. CASEY, REV. JAMES V., J.C.D., A Study of Canon 2222 § 1, XII-127 pp., 1949.
291. ALLGEIER, REV. JOSEPH L., J.C.D., The Canonical Obligation of Preaching in Parish Churches, X-115 pp., 1949 (printed 1950).
292. CAHILL, REV. DANIEL R., J.C.D., The Custody of the Holy Eucharist, XVI-178 pp., 1949 (printed 1950).
293. CARR, REV. AIDEN, A.F.M., CARM., S.T.D., J.C.D., Vocation to the Priesthood: Its Canonical Concept.
294. KNOPKE, REV. ROCH F., O.F.M., J.C.D., Reverential Fear in Matrimonial Cases in Asiatic Countries: Rota Cases, XII-112 pp., 1949.
295. LAVELLE, REV. HOWARD D., J.C.D., The Obligation of Holding Sacred Missions in Parishes, XVI-142 pp., 1949.
296. MICKELLS, REV. ANTHONY B., J.C.D., The Constitutive Elements of Parishes.
297. NOONE, REV. JOHN J., J.C.D., Nullity in Judicial Acts, X-147 pp., 1949 (printed 1950).
298. SHEEHAN, REV. DANIEL E., J.C.D., The Minister of Holy Communion.
299. STATKUS, REV. FRANCIS J., J.C.D., The Minister of the Last Sacraments.
300. COOK, REV. JOHN P., J.C.D., Ecclesiastical Communities and Their Ability to Induce Legal Customs, XII-152 pp., 1949 (printed (1950).
301. FAZZALARO, REV. FRANCIS J., J.C.D., The Place for the Hearing of Confessions, X-150 pp., 1949 (printed 1950).
302. HANNAN, REV. PHILIP M., J.C.D., The Canonical Concept of *congrua sustentatio* for the Secular Clergy, XII-237 pp., 1949 (printed 1950).

*For a complete list of the available numbers of this series apply to the Catholic University of America Press, 620 Michigan Ave., N. E., Washington 17, D. C., for a general catalogue.

303. QUINN, REV. HUGH G., S.T.L., J.C.D., The Particular Penal Precept.
304. GALLAGHER, REV. JOHN F., J.C.D., The Matrimonial Impediment of Public Propriety.
305. WELSH, REV. THOMAS J., J.C.D., The Use of the Portable Altar.
306. WATERS, REV. JOSEPH L., S.S.J., J.C.D., The Probation in Societies of Quasi-Religious.
307. REGAN, REV. MICHAEL J., J.C.D., Canon 16.
308. BYRNE, REV. HARRY J., J.C.L., Investment of Church Funds.
309. GALLAGHER, REV. THOMAS V., J.C.D., The Rejection of Judicial Witnesses and Testimony.
310. CHATHAM, REV. JOSIAH G., PH.B., S.T.L., J.C.D., Force and Fear as Invalidating Marriage: the Element of Injustice, XIV-183 pp., 1950.

www.ingramcontent.com/pod-product-compliance
Lightning Source LLC
LaVergne TN
LVHW050222080826
844660LV00012B/452

* 9 7 8 0 8 1 3 2 2 4 8 3 1 *